AF255896

Climbing a Few of Japan's 100 Famous Mountains –

Volume 2:
Mt. Chokai (Choukai)

Daniel H. Wieczorek and Kazuya Numazawa

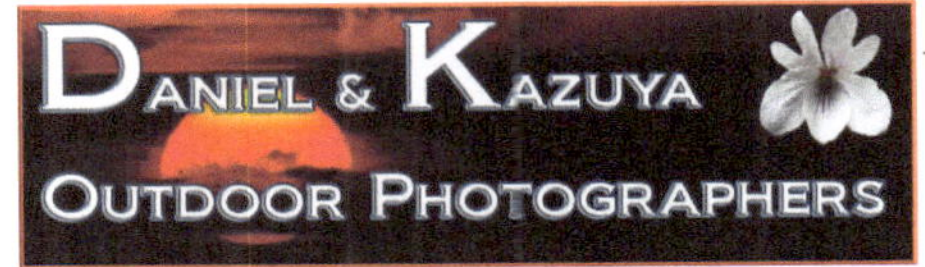

Climbing a Few of Japan's 100 Famous Mountains –
Volume 2:
Mt. Chokai (Mt. Choukai)

DEDICATION

This work is dedicated, first of all, to my partner, Kazuya Numazawa. He always keeps my interest in photography up and makes me keep striving for the perfect photo. He also often makes me think of the expression "when the going gets tough, the tough keep going." Without my partner it has to also be noted that I most likely would not have climbed any of these mountains.

Secondly, it is dedicated to my mother and father, bless them, for tolerating and even encouraging my photography hobby from the time I was twelve years old.

And, finally, it is dedicated to my friends who have encouraged me to create books of photographs which I have taken while doing mountain climbing.

Other Books in this Series

"Climbing a Few of Japan's 100 Famous Mountains – Volume 1: Mt. Daisetsu (Mt. Asahidake)"; ISBN-13: 9781493777204; 66 Pages; Dec. 5, 2013

"Climbing a Few of Japan's 100 Famous Mountains – Volume 3: Mt. Gassan"; ISBN-13: 9781494872175; 70 Pages; January 4, 2014

"Climbing a Few of Japan's 100 Famous Mountains – Volume 4: Mt. Hakkoda & Mt. Zao"; ISBN-13: 9781495396564; 88 Pages; Jan. 31, 2014

"Climbing a Few of Japan's 100 Famous Mountains – Volume 5: Mt. Kumotori"; ISBN-13: 9781495980527; 84 Pages; February 17, 2014

"A Pocket-Size Version of Climbing a Few of Japan's 100 Famous Mountains – Volume 5: Mt. Kumotori"; ISBN-13: 9781497444942; 90 Pages; March 25, 2014

"Climbing a Few of Japan's 100 Famous Mountains – Volume 6: Mt. Shirane (Kusatsu)"; ISBN-13: 9781497303232; 80 Pages; March 11, 2014

"Climbing a Few of Japan's 100 Famous Mountains – Volume 7: Mt. Shibutsu"; ISBN-13: 9781497539273; 80 Pages; April 4, 2014

"Climbing a Few of Japan's 100 Famous Mountains – Volume 8: Mt. Kiso-Komagatake"; ISBN-13: 9781499178630; 72 Pages; April 18, 2014

"Climbing a Few of Japan's 100 Famous Mountains – Volume 9: Mt. Kitadake"; ISBN-13: 9781499786088; 62 Pages; June 4, 2014

"Climbing a Few of Japan's 100 Famous Mountains – Volume 10: Mt. Mizugaki"; ISBN-13: 9781500235284; 70 Pages; June 18, 2014

"Climbing a Few of Japan's 100 Famous Mountains – Volume 11: Mt. Shiroumadake (includes Mt. Shakushidake & Mt. Yarigatake)"; ISBN-13: 9781500463885; 178 Pages; July 9, 2014

"Climbing a Few of Japan's 100 Famous Mountains – Volume 12: Mt. Tate (Tateyama)"; ISBN-13: 9781500946326; 176 Pages; Aug. 26, 2014

"Climbing a Few of Japan's 100 Famous Mountains – Volume 13: Mt. Yatsugatake (Mt. Akadake)"; ISBN-13: 9781502877581; 208 Pages; October 22, 2014

FOREWORD

What is the purpose of this series of books? It is to show you, in photographs, some of the astounding sights and scenery we have seen while climbing the mountains included herein. At this time we have climbed 14 of Japan's 100 Famous Mountains. The ones we have climbed are: 1) Mt. Daisetsu (2,290 m) (大雪山) = Mt. Asahidake (旭岳); 2) Mt. Chokai (2,236 m) (鳥海山); 3) Mt. Gassan (1,984 m) (月山); 4) Mt. Hakkoda (1,584 m) (八甲田山); 5) Mt. Zao (1,841 m) (蔵王山); 6) Mt. Kumotori (2,017 m) (雲取山); 7) Mt. Kusatsu-Shirane (2,171 m) (草津白根山); 8) Mt. Shibutsu (2,228 m) (至仏山); 9) Mt. Kiso-Komagatake (2,956 m) (木曾駒ヶ岳); 10) Mt. Kitadake (North Peak) (3,192 m) (北岳); 11) Mt. Mizugaki (2,230 m) (瑞牆山); 12) Mt. Shiroumadake (2,932 m) (白馬岳); 13) Mt. Tateyama (3,015 m) (立山); and 14) Mt. Yatsugatake (2,899 m) (八ヶ岳).

By the way, I (Daniel) did all of the writing and Kazuya did a fair percentage of the photography. So, do not be surprised from time to time when you see references such as "Kazuya" and "that's me…".

Daniel and Kazuya's ***"Outdoor Photography of Japan: Through the Seasons"*** includes some of the same photos as this work, but this work may be thought of as a subset of that work because that work includes adventures to many mountains beyond the 14 famous mountains which are found in this series of books. In addition, the photos in that book were more than 50% flower photos. This series includes less than 1% flower photos, and only where the flower is a part of a mountain scene. In addition, the majority of the photos you'll find in this series were not included in that work.

TABLE OF CONTENTS

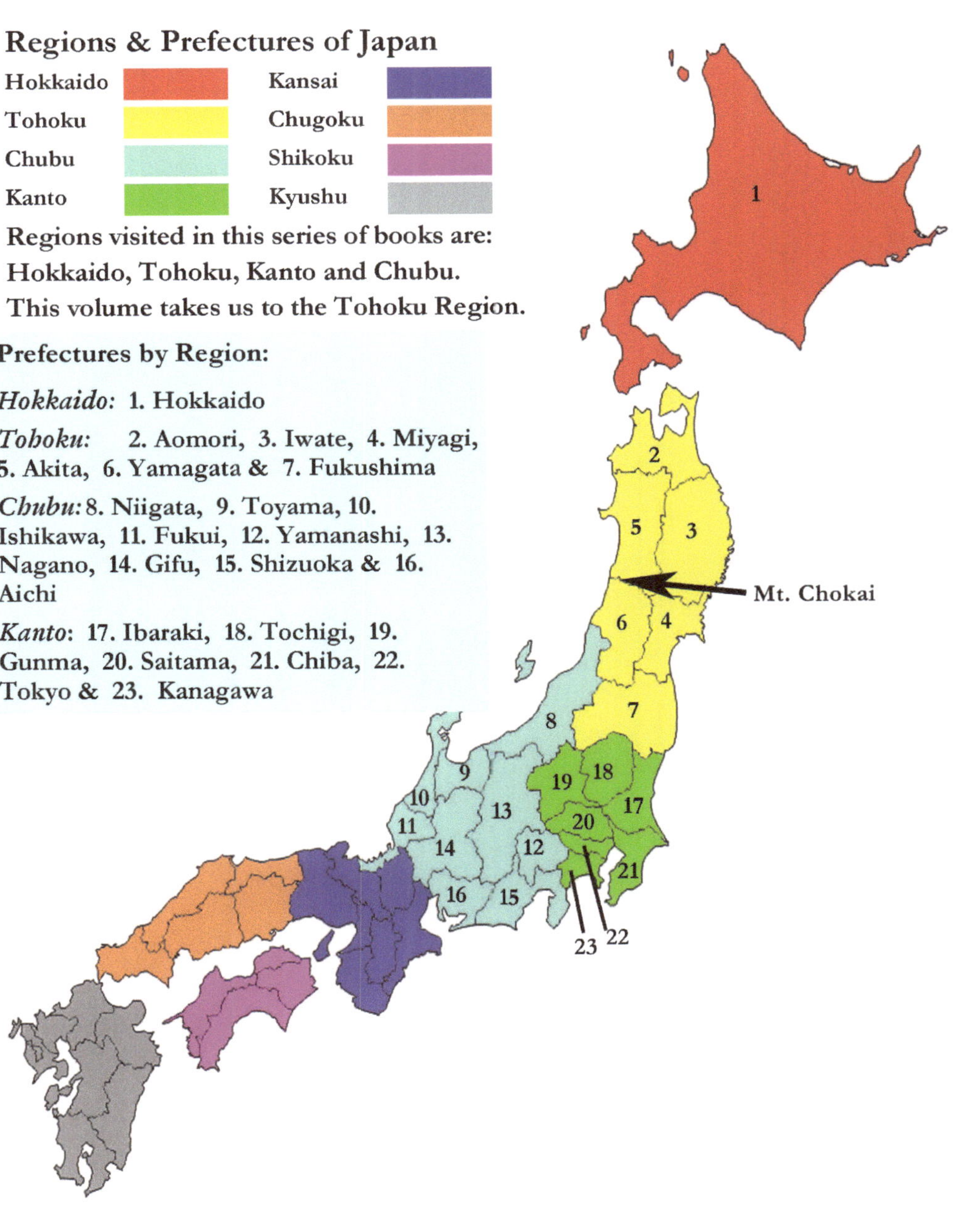

Regions & Prefectures of Japan

Hokkaido Kansai
Tohoku Chugoku
Chubu Shikoku
Kanto Kyushu

Regions visited in this series of books are:
Hokkaido, Tohoku, Kanto and Chubu.
This volume takes us to the Tohoku Region.

Prefectures by Region:

Hokkaido: 1. Hokkaido

Tohoku: 2. Aomori, 3. Iwate, 4. Miyagi,
5. Akita, 6. Yamagata & 7. Fukushima

Chubu: 8. Niigata, 9. Toyama, 10.
Ishikawa, 11. Fukui, 12. Yamanashi, 13.
Nagano, 14. Gifu, 15. Shizuoka & 16.
Aichi

Kanto: 17. Ibaraki, 18. Tochigi, 19.
Gunma, 20. Saitama, 21. Chiba, 22.
Tokyo & 23. Kanagawa

1) JAPAN'S 100 FAMOUS MOUNTAINS

What are Japan's 100 famous mountains? A selection of famous mountains in Japan has been compiled since the Edo period (1603 – 1867) and the list has been revised several times since the very first list appeared. At the current time the list of 100 famous mountains includes those shown below. Also shown is the Japanese pronunciation, elevation in meters and feet, the Japanese kanji, the Region the mountain is in and a few a.k.a. (also known as) names.

Hokkaido:

1.	Mt. Akan (Akandake)	1,499	4,918	阿寒岳
2.	**Mt. Asahi (Asahidake) a.k.a.**			
	Mt. Daisetsu (Daisetsuzan)	**2,290**	**7,513**	**旭岳**
	a.k.a. (大雪山)			
3.	Mt. Poroshiri (Poroshiridake)	2,052	6,734	幌尻岳
4.	Mt. Rausu (Rausudake)	1,660	5,446	羅臼岳
5.	Mt. Rishiri (Rishiridake)	1,721	5,646	利尻岳
6.	Mt. Shari (Sharidake)	1,545	5,069	斜里岳
7.	Mt. Tokachi (Tochidake)	2,077	6,814	十勝岳
8.	Mt. Tomuraushi (Tomuraushiyama)	2,141	7,024	
	トムラウシ山			
9.	Mt. Yotei (Yoteizan) a.k.a.			
	(Mt. Shiribeshi) (Shiribeshiyama)	1,893	6,211	羊蹄山
	a.k.a. (後方羊蹄山)			

Tohoku Region:

10.	Mt. Adatara (Adatarayama)	1,700	5,577	
	安達太良山			
11.	Mt. Aizu-Komagatake (Aizukomagatake)			
		2,132	6,995	会津駒ケ岳
12.	Mt. Asahi (Asahirenpou)	1,870	6,135	朝日連峰
13.	Mt. Azuma (Azumayama)	2,035	6,676	吾妻山
14.	Mt. Bandai (Bandaisan)	1,819	5,968	磐梯山
15.	**Mt. Chōkai (Chōkaisan)**	**2,236**	**7,336**	**鳥海山**
16.	**Mt. Gassan (Gassan)**	**1,984**	**6,509**	**月山**
17.	Mt. Hachimantai (Hachimantai)	1,614	5,295	八幡平
18.	**Mt. Hakkōda (Hakkōdasan)**	**1,584**	**5,197**	**八甲田山**

19.	Mt. Hayachine (Hayachinesan)	1,917	6,289	早池峰山
20.	Mt. Hiuchigatake (Hiuchigatake)	2,356	7,730	燧ケ岳
21.	Mt. Iide (Iiderenpou)	2,105	6,906	飯豊連峰
22.	Mt. Iwaki (Iwakisan)	1,625	5,331	岩木山
23.	Mt. Iwate (Iwatesan)	2,038	6,686	岩手山
24.	**Mt. Zaō (Zaōsan)**	**1,841**	**6,040**	**蔵王山**

Kanto Region:

25.	Mt. Akagi (Akagiyama)	1,828	5,997	赤城山
26.	Mt. Asama (Asamayama)	2,568	8,425	浅間山
27.	Mt. Azumaya (Azumayasan)	2,354	7,723	四阿山
28.	Mt. Hiragatake (Hiragatake)	2,141	7,024	平ヶ岳
29.	Mt. Hotaka (Hotakayama)	2,158	7,080	武尊山
30.	**Mt. Kumotori (Kumotoriyama)**	**2,017**	**6,617**	**雲取山**
31.	**Mt. Kusatsu-Shirane (Kusatsu-Shiranesan)**	**2,171**	**7,123**	**草津白根山**
32.	Mt. Nantai (Nantaisan)	2,486	8,156	男体山
33.	Mt. Nasu (Nasudake)	1,915	6,283	那須岳
34.	Mt. Nikko-Shirane (Nikko-Shiranesan)	2,578	8,458	日光白根山
35.	Mt. Ryokami (Ryoukamisan)	1,723	5,653	両神山
36.	**Mt. Shibutsu (Shibutsusan)**	**2,228**	**7,310**	**至仏山**
37.	Mt. Sukai (Sukaisan)	2,144	7,034	皇海山
38.	Mt. Tanigawa (Tanigawadake)	1,963	6,440	谷川岳
39.	Mt. Tanzawa (Tanzawasan)	1,567	5,141	丹沢山
40.	Mt. Tsukuba (Tsukubasan)	877	2,877	筑波山

Chubu Region:

41.	Mt. Ainodake (Ainodake)	3,189	10,463	間ノ岳
42.	Mt. Akaishi (Akaishidake)	3,120	10,236	赤石岳
43.	Mt. Amagi (Amagisan)	1,406	4,613	天城山
44.	Mt. Amakazari (Amakazariyama)	1,963	6,440	雨飾山
45.	Mt. Daibosatsu (Daibosatsurei)	2,057	6,749	大菩薩嶺
46.	Mt. Ena (Enasan)	2,191	7,188	恵那山
47.	Mt. Fuji (Fujisan)	3,776	12,388	富士山
48.	Mt. Goryū (Goryūdake)	2,814	9,232	五竜岳
49.	Mt. Hakusan (Hakusan)	2,702	8,865	白山
50.	Mt. Hijiri (Hijiridake)	3,013	9,885	聖岳
51.	Mt. Hiuchi (Hiuchiyama)	2,462	8,077	火打山
52.	Mt. Hōō (Hōōsan)	2,840	9,318	鳳凰山

		ft	m	
53.	Mt. Hotaka (Hotakadake)	3,190	10,466	穂高岳
54.	Mt. Jōnen (Jōnendake)	2,857	9,373	常念岳
55.	Mt. Kai-Komagatake (Kaikomagatake)	2,967	9,734	甲斐駒ケ岳
56.	Mt. Kasa (Kasagatake)	2,897	9,505	笠ヶ岳
57.	Mt. Kashima Yarigatake (Kashimayarigatake)	2,889	9,478	鹿島槍ヶ岳
58.	Mt. Kinpu (Kinpusan)	2,599	8,527	金峰山
59.	Mt. Kirigamine (Kirigamine)	1,925	6,316	霧ヶ峰
60.	**Mt. Kiso-Komagatake (Kisokomagatake)**	**2,956**	**9,698**	**木曽駒ケ岳**
61.	**Mt. Kitadake (Kitadake)**	**3,192**	**10,472**	**北岳**
62.	Mt. Kobushi (Kobushidake)	2,475	8,120	甲武信岳
63.	Mt. Kuro (Kurodake) a.k.a. (Mt. Suisho) (Suishodake)	2,978	9,770	黒岳 a.k.a. (水晶岳)
64.	Mt. Kurobe-Gorō (Kurobegorōdake)	2,840	9,318	黒部五郎岳
65.	Mt. Makihata (Makihatayama)	1,967	6,453	巻機山
66.	**Mt. Mizugaki (Mizugakiyama)**	**2,230**	**7,316**	**瑞牆山**
67.	Mt. Myoko (Myokosan)	2,454	8,051	妙高山
68.	Mt. Naeba (Naebasan)	2,145	7,037	苗場山
69.	Mt. Norikura (Norikuradake)	3,026	9,928	乗鞍岳
70.	Mt. Ontake (Ontakesan)	3,067	10,062	御嶽山
71.	Mt. Senjōgatake (Senjōgatake)	3,033	9,951	仙丈ケ岳
72.	Mt. Shiomi (Shiomidake)	3,047	9,997	塩見岳
73.	**Mt. Shiroumadake (Shiroumadake)**	**2,932**	**9,619**	**白馬岳**
74.	Mt. Takatsuma (Takatsumayama)	2,353	7,720	高妻山
75.	Mt. Tateshina (Tateshinayama)	2,530	8,301	蓼科山
76.	**Mt. Tateyama (Tateyama)**	**3,015**	**9,892**	**立山**
77.	Mt. Tekari (Tekaridake)	2,591	8,501	光岳
78.	Mt. Tsurugi (Tsurugidake)	2,999	9,839	劔岳
79.	Mt. Uonuma-Komagatake a.k.a. (Echigo-Komagatake)	2,003	6,572	魚沼駒ヶ岳 a.k.a. (越後駒ケ岳)
80.	Mt. Utsugi (Utsugidake)	2,864	9,396	空木岳
81.	Mt. Warusawa (Warusawadake)	3,141	10,305	悪沢岳
82.	Mt. Washiba (Washibadake)	2,924	9,593	鷲羽岳
83.	Mt. Yake (Yakedake)	2,444	8,018	焼岳

84.	Mt. Yakushi (Yakushidake)	2,926	9,600	薬師岳
85.	Mt. Yarigatake (Yarigatake)	3,180	10,433	槍ヶ岳
86.	**Mt. Yatsugatake (Yatsugatake)**	**2,899**	**9,511**	**八ヶ岳**
87.	Utsukushigahara Highland (Utsukushigahara)	2,034	6,673	美ヶ原

Western Japan:

88.	Mt. Arashima (Arashimadake)	1,523	4,997	荒島岳
89.	Mt. Aso (Asosan)	1,592	5,223	阿蘇山
90.	Mt. Daisen (Daisen)	1,729	5,673	大山
91.	Mt. Ibuki (Ibukiyama)	1,377	4,518	伊吹山
92.	Mt. Ishizuchi (Ishizuchisan)	1,982	6,503	石鎚山
93.	Mt. Kaimon (Kaimondake)	924	3,031	開聞岳
94.	Mt. Kirishima (Kirishimayama)	1,700	5,577	霧島山
95.	Mt. Kujū (Kujūsan)	1,791	5,876	九重山
96.	Mt. Miya-no-ura (Miyanouradake)	1,936	6,352	宮之浦岳
97.	Mt. Ōmine (Ōminesan)	1,915	6,283	大峰山
98.	Mt. Sobo (Sobosan)	1,756	5,761	祖母山
99.	Mt. Tsurugi (Tsurugisan)	1,955	6,414	剣山
100.	The Wide Mountain of Ōdai (Ōdaigaharayama)	1,695	5,561	大台ケ原山

My partner and I have climbed (or in one, case merely ascended) the fourteen mountains which are **shaded, underlined and in bold** text. You'll probably note that we have not climbed Mt. Fuji and wonder why? The reason is simple – too many people and not enough interesting sights.

Using photographs and a minimum amount of text we are telling (showing) you the stories of climbing the 14 mountains shown above. We started at the beginning of the 100 mountains list and are working our way through it. That means that the first climb we showed you, in Volume 1, was on Hokkaido and it was a climb of Mt. Daisetsu (2,290.9 m = 7,516 ft) (大雪山), which is also known as Mt. Asahi-dake. Mt. Daisetsu is the name of the entire mountain range, while Mount Asahi (旭岳 Asahidake) is the tallest mountain in that mountain range and also the tallest mountain in Hokkaido Prefecture, Japan. It is part of the Daisetsuzan Volcanic Group and it is located in the northern part of Daisetsuzan National Park.

The second mountain we'll show you, here in Volume 2, is in the Tohoku Region and the mountain name is Mt. Chokai (or Choukai) (2,236 m = 7,336 ft) (鳥海山). Mt. Chokai is located on the southern border of Akita Prefecture and the northern border of Yamagata Prefecture. It is still an active volcano (most recent eruption – 1974) and it is the second tallest mountain in the Tohoku Region of Japan.

The third mountain is also in the Tohoku Region and it is Mt. Gassan (1,984 m = 6,509 ft) (月山). Mt. Gassan is the highest peak in the Dewa Sanzan trio of sacred mountains. It lies between Mt. Chokai to the north, and Mt. Asahi to the south, in Yamagata Prefecture. Being a sacred mountain, it is famous for the shrine at the summit and in the summer you can often see large groups of white-clothed pilgrims hiking to or from the summit.

The fourth mountain we will show you is also in the Tohoku Region of Japan and the mountain will be Mt. Hakkoda (1,584 m = 5,197 ft) (八甲田山). The Hakkoda Mountains are a volcanic mountain range that lie south of Aomori City, in Aomori Prefecture Japan. The peak name is actually Mt. Hakkoda – Odake. Odake is the tallest peak in the Hakkoda Range.

The fifth mountain we'll show you is Mt. Zao (1,841 m = 6,040 ft) (蔵王山). It is also in the Tohoku Region and also in Yamagata Prefecture. We did not actually make it to the summit of this mountain. We visited it in the winter and it was very cold and windy. We took an automobile as far as possible and then transferred to a gondola car and went only a little bit beyond the top of the gondola – to about the 1,661 m (= 5,449 ft) level of the mountain. We do, however, have some impressive photos from that trip.

The sixth mountain you'll see in this series of books will be Mt. Kumotori (2,017.7 m = 6,620 ft) (雲取山). This is in the Kanto Region and the peak divides the prefectures of Tokyo, Yamanashi and Saitama. Its summit is the highest point in Tokyo. It separates the Okutama Mountains and the Okuchichibu Mountains. No matter which direction you choose to come to this mountain from, the summit is a long hike from the nearest bus stop, road end or train station.

The seventh mountain will be Mt. Kusatsu-Shirane (2,171 m = 7,123 ft) (草津白根山). This peak is also in the Kanto Region of Japan, in Gunma Prefecture. It is called Mt. Kusatsu-Shirane to differentiate it from Mt. Nikko-Shirane, which is on the opposite side of Gunma Prefecture. There is a beautifully colored volcanic pond here known as Yugama. Another volcanic pond close-by is Yumiike and there is a dry crater named Karagama Crater.

The eighth mountain, also in the Kanto Region, in Gunma Prefecture, will be Mt. Shibutsu (2,228 m = 7,310 ft) (至仏山). It separates Oze Marsh (Oze National Park) from the remainder of Gunma Prefecture. It is an interesting mountain composed primarily of serpentinite. There is also a lesser peak known as Mt. Koshibutsu (2,162 m = 7,093 ft).

The ninth mountain we'll take you to is Mt. Kiso-Komagatake (2,956 m = 9,698 ft) (木曾駒ヶ岳). It can be found in Nagano Prefecture, in the Chubu Region. It is located in Japan's Central Alps Mountain Range and is the highest peak in that range.

Then we'll very briefly take you to the tenth of Japan's 100 famous mountains which we have climbed – Mt. Kitadake (North Peak) (3,193 m = 10,476 ft) (北岳). This is Japan's second highest mountain after Mt. Fuji and is known as "the Leader of the Southern Alps". It is in Yamanashi Prefecture, in the Chubu Region.

Mt. Mizugaki (2,230 m = 7,317 ft) (瑞牆山) is the eleventh mountain that will be addressed in this series of books. It too is in the Chubu Region. It is in Yamanashi Prefecture. It lies across the valley from the Southern Alps, slightly southeast of Yatsugatake and northwest of the Daibosatsu ridgeline. Granite towers, blocks and obelisks protrude from the summit of this mountains. It is truly an amazing sight to see from its lower slopes.

Then we'll continue on to the twelfth mountain and that is also in the Chubu Region. It is Mt. Shiroumadake (2,932 m = 9,620 ft) (白馬岳). It is the tallest peak in the Hakuba section of the Hida Mountains, also known as Japan's Northern Alps Mountain Range. It is in Nagano Prefecture.

After that, for the thirteenth mountain, we'll take you to another Chubu Region mountain – Mt. Tateyama (3,015 m = 9,892 ft) (立山). It can be found in the southeastern portion of Toyama Prefecture and it also is a mountain in the Northern Alps Mountain Range, or Hida Mountains. It is one of the tallest peaks in the Hida Mountains and is the highest peak in Toyama Prefecture.

The fourteenth and final mountain we'll cover in this series of books is also in the Chubu Region – Mt. Yatsugatake (Mt. Akadake – 2,899 m = 9,511 ft) (八ヶ岳). Yatsugatake means "eight peaks" and the highest mountain in this range is Mt. Akadake. Actually there are many more than eight peaks, but in Japanese the kanji character for Hachi (八) sometimes implies "many" or "several.

According to legend, Yatsugatake was once higher than Mount Fuji, but Konohana-Sakuyahime, the goddess of Mount Fuji, tore it down out of jealousy, leaving the collection of peaks we have today. This could possibly be true considering that Yatsugatake is older than Fuji and as Fuji rose in prominence Yatsugatake wore away.

Another version of this legend says that a long time ago, Yatsugatake was an ordinary mountain with only one peak, and it was as high as or higher then Mt. Fuji. Yatsugatake's god and Mt. Fuji's goddess began quarreling over their height. Each of them insisted that he/she was taller. The Amitabha Buddha, who was entrusted to arbitrate the dispute, set a valley between the tops of the two mountains and filled it with water. The water submerged the summit of Mt. Fuji, revealing that Yatsugatake was indeed, taller. Mt. Fuji's goddess, who was unyielding, was very angry so she kept striking Yatsugatake with a long stick until it was divided into several peaks, all lower than Mt. Fuji. That is why Mt. Yatsugatake now has so many peaks. Interesting!

By the way – *dake* or *take* (岳) = peak or high peak. Some authors prefer to leave this term off when referring to a Japanese mountain, for example they will refer to Mt. Kitadake as Mt. Kita and use the argument that it is redundant to use the –dake portion of the name. We prefer to use the dake suffix for completeness. If one is to be absolutely correct it should probably be called Kita Peak, not Mt. Kita.

"Mountains are the cathedrals where I practice my religion."
— Anatoli Boukreev

"Climb the mountains and get their good tidings. Nature's peace will flow into you as sunshine flows into trees. The winds will blow their own freshness into you, and the storms their energy, while cares will drop away from you like the leaves of Autumn."
— John Muir, The Mountains of California

"Chasing angels or fleeing demons, go to the mountains."
— Jeffrey Rasley

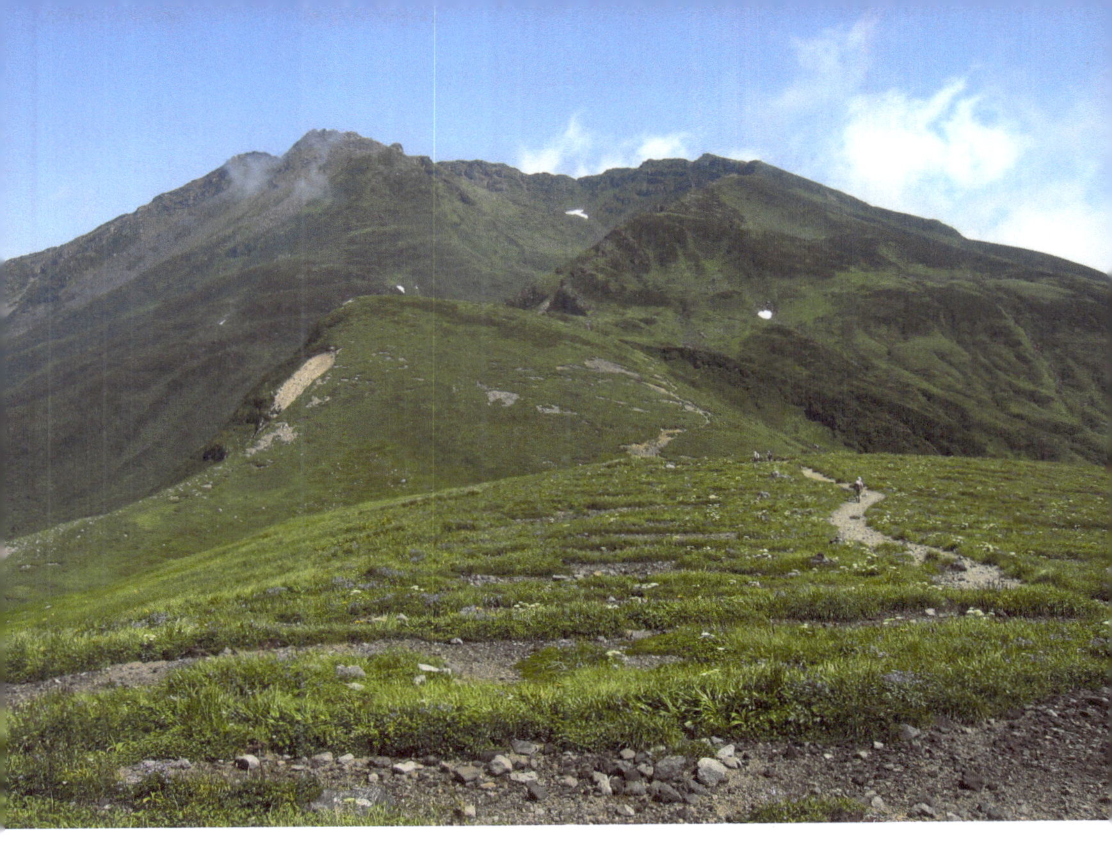

2) Mt. Chokai (Choukai)

This is the second climb that we are showing you in this series of books. It is a climb of Mt. Chokai (= Mt. Choukai) (2,236 m = 7,336 ft) (鳥海山). Mt. Chokai is in the Tohoku Region of Japan and lies on the Northern Boundary of Yamagata Prefecture and the Southern Boundary of Akita Prefecture. It is still an active volcano and it is the second tallest mountain in the Tohoku Region of Japan. It last erupted in March and April, 1974.

We have climbed Mt. Chokai three times. Our first time was on August 11, 2005, our second time was on August 9, 2008 and our third time was on August 8, 2011. We stayed for only one night all three times, in the hut which is located on the very first flatter spot below the summit. From the hut to the summit of the mountain is a scramble over huge volcanic boulders and takes about twenty-five minutes. We experienced a lot of rain on our first climb, only a little on our second climb and no rain at all on our third climb.

We are not precisely sure how to go about telling the story of these climbs. Would it be better to do it by year or would it be better to just show the best photographs in order from the base of the mountain to the summit and then the descent back to the starting point? Attempting to take your desires into account, maybe the best way is to show all three sets of photos and identify each photo as to the year it was taken. By doing it that way you will be able to see the contrasts between the various types of weather without having to flip back and forth between pages of 2005, 2008 and 2011 photographs. It seems clumsy to have to say things like "for a clear weather scene of this area please see page whatever".

The first photo above was taken during our 2008 climb and it shows the upper portion of Mt. Chokai only. It includes the summit and it was taken from a plateau area which you will come to after about two to three hours of climbing.

On the facing page is a map of this mountain and the previous photo was taken approximately at the point marked 1. on the map.

The following image is a 3-shot panorama which shows the same area as the previous photo, but it shows a greater area to both sides of the peak.

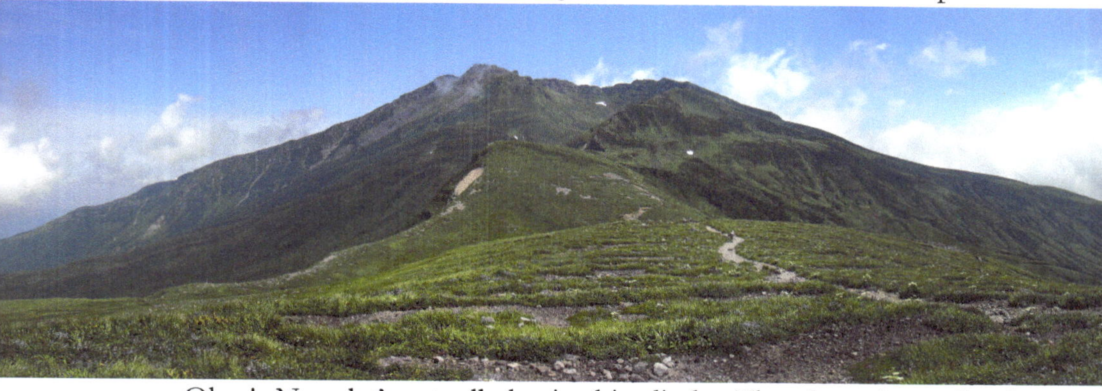

Okay! Now let's actually begin this climb. The photo immediately below shows the parking area and the visitor center at the start of the climb, which is called Hokodate. As you can see, the parking area is plenty large enough for several cars. You will also note that there is a bus there – it is possible to take a bus from the city of Sakata to here. In addition, from the town of Kisakata you can take a mini-bus and that bus gets you here early enough so that you can start climbing at around 7:30 AM. It takes us about seven hours to climb from here to the summit – you may be able to do it quicker.

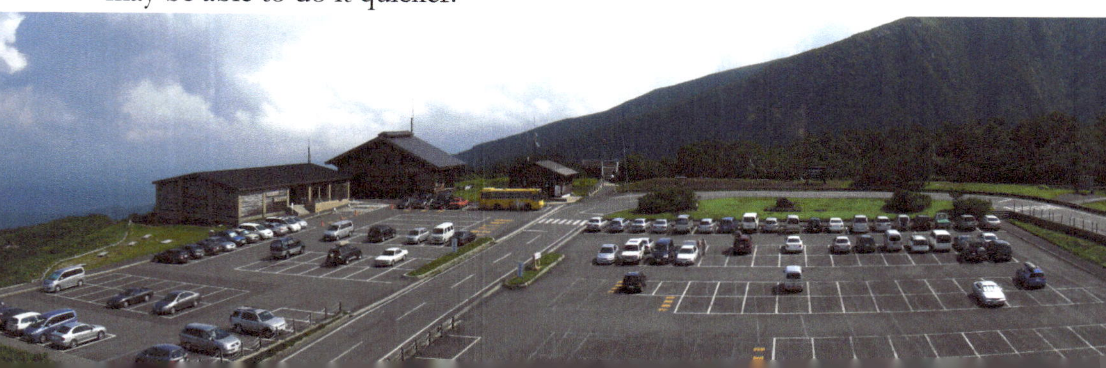

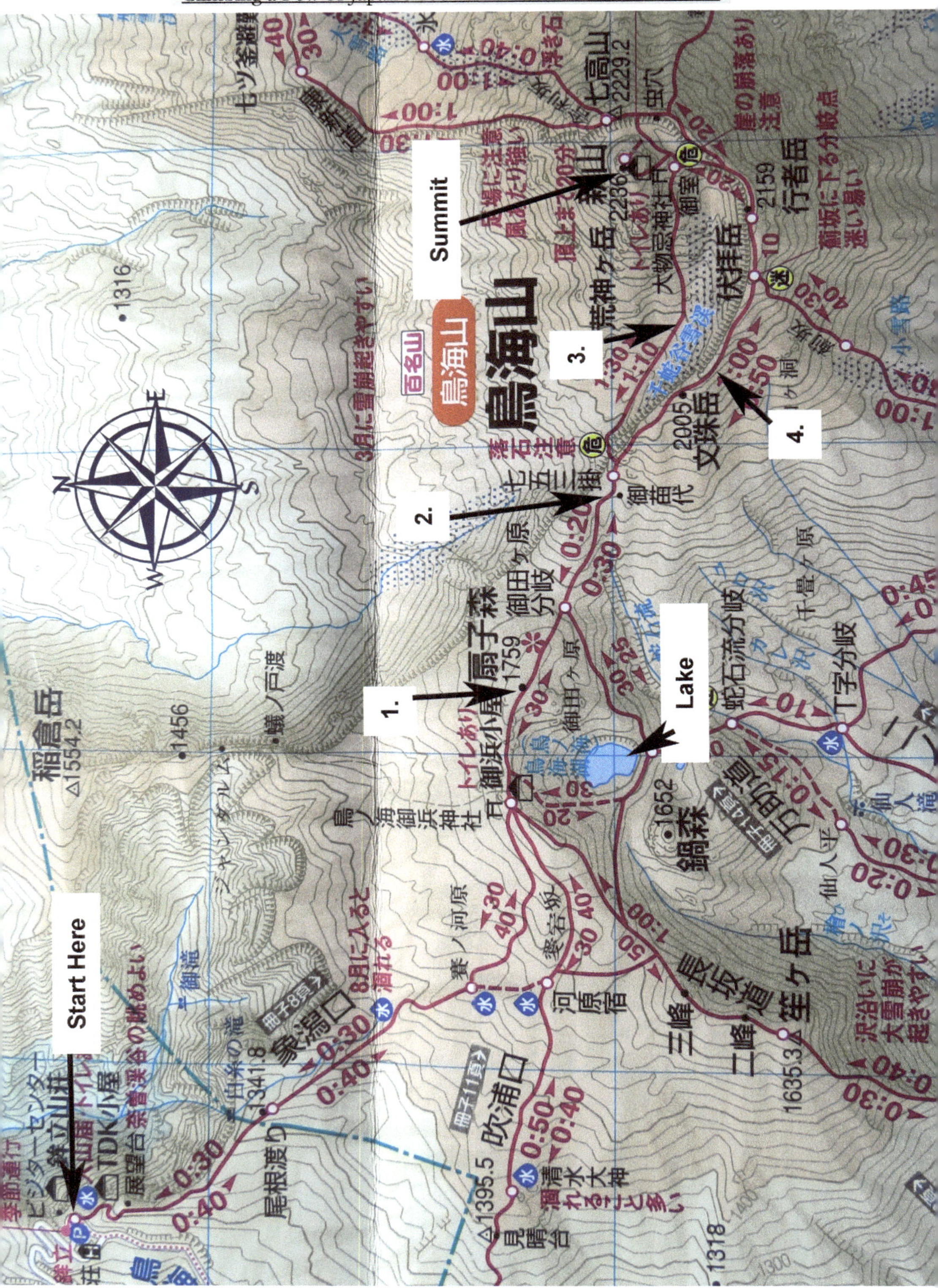

Summit
鳥海山
百名山
鳥海山
1.
2.
3.
4.
Lake
Start Here

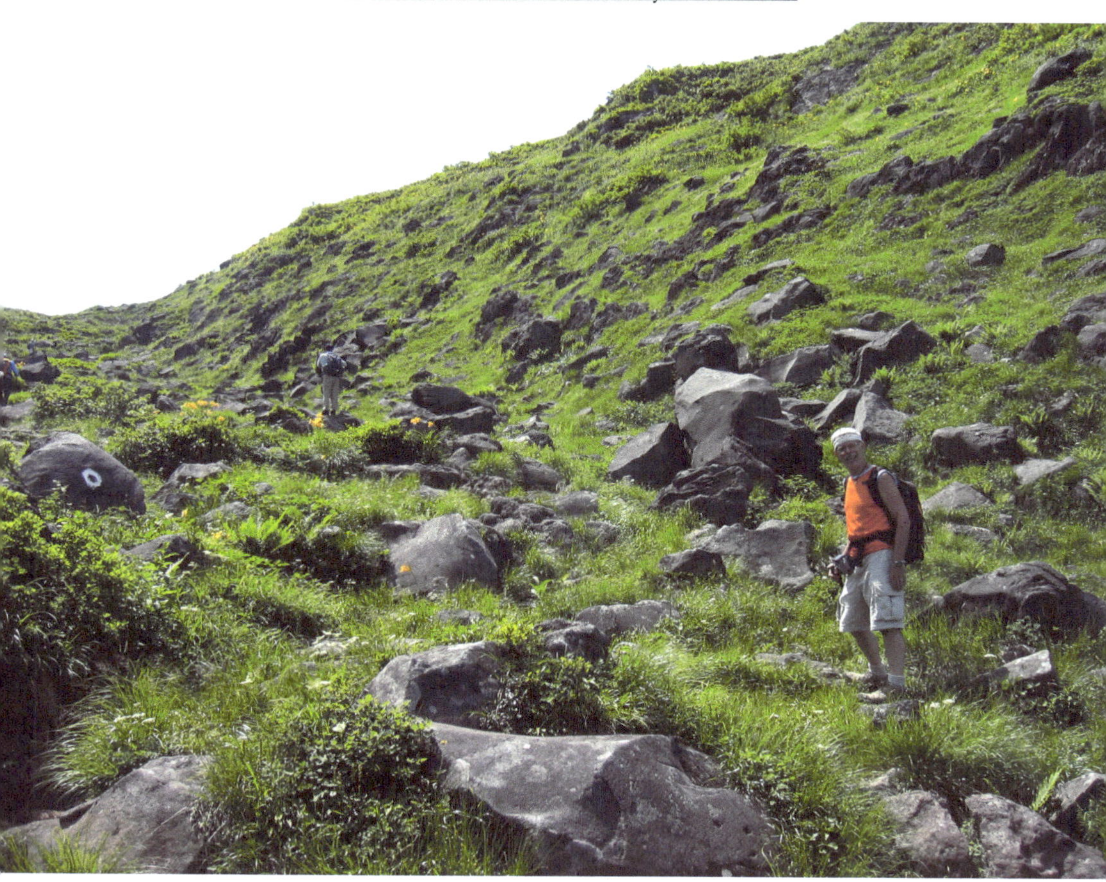

The photo above shows the lower slopes, but after one is well above the starting point. The person on the right side of the photo is me. Near the left side of the photo you can see a circle painted on one of the large rocks – that is how the trail is marked.

The top photo on the facing page is another shot which was taken as we climbed up to the first hut which you can see on the map (north of the "Lake" annotation). Note how incredibly green the slopes are.

The lower photo on the facing page gives you one more shot of this general area between the starting point and the first hut shown on the map. In this photo you should note not only the amazing green, but also all of the mountain lilies.

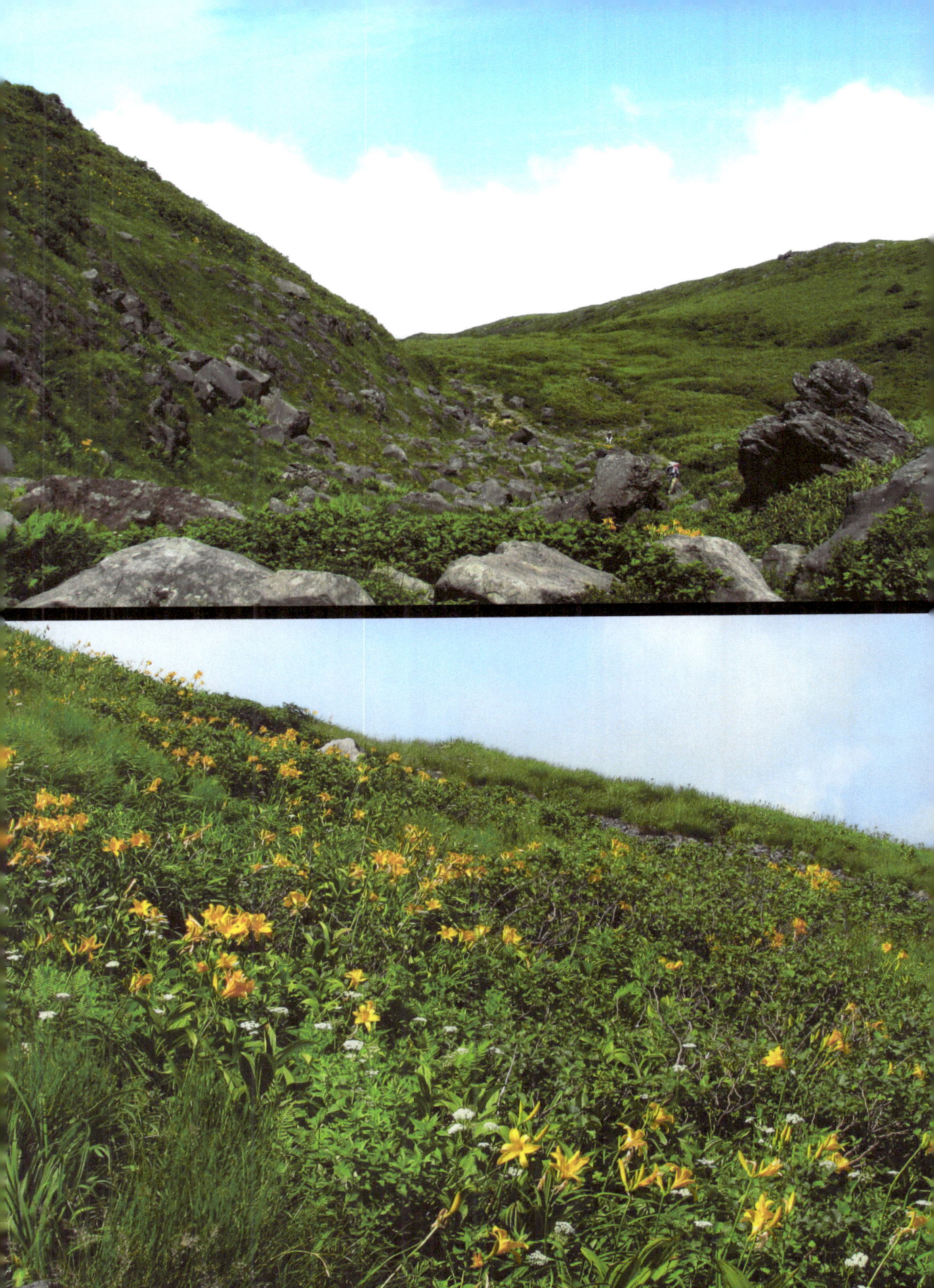

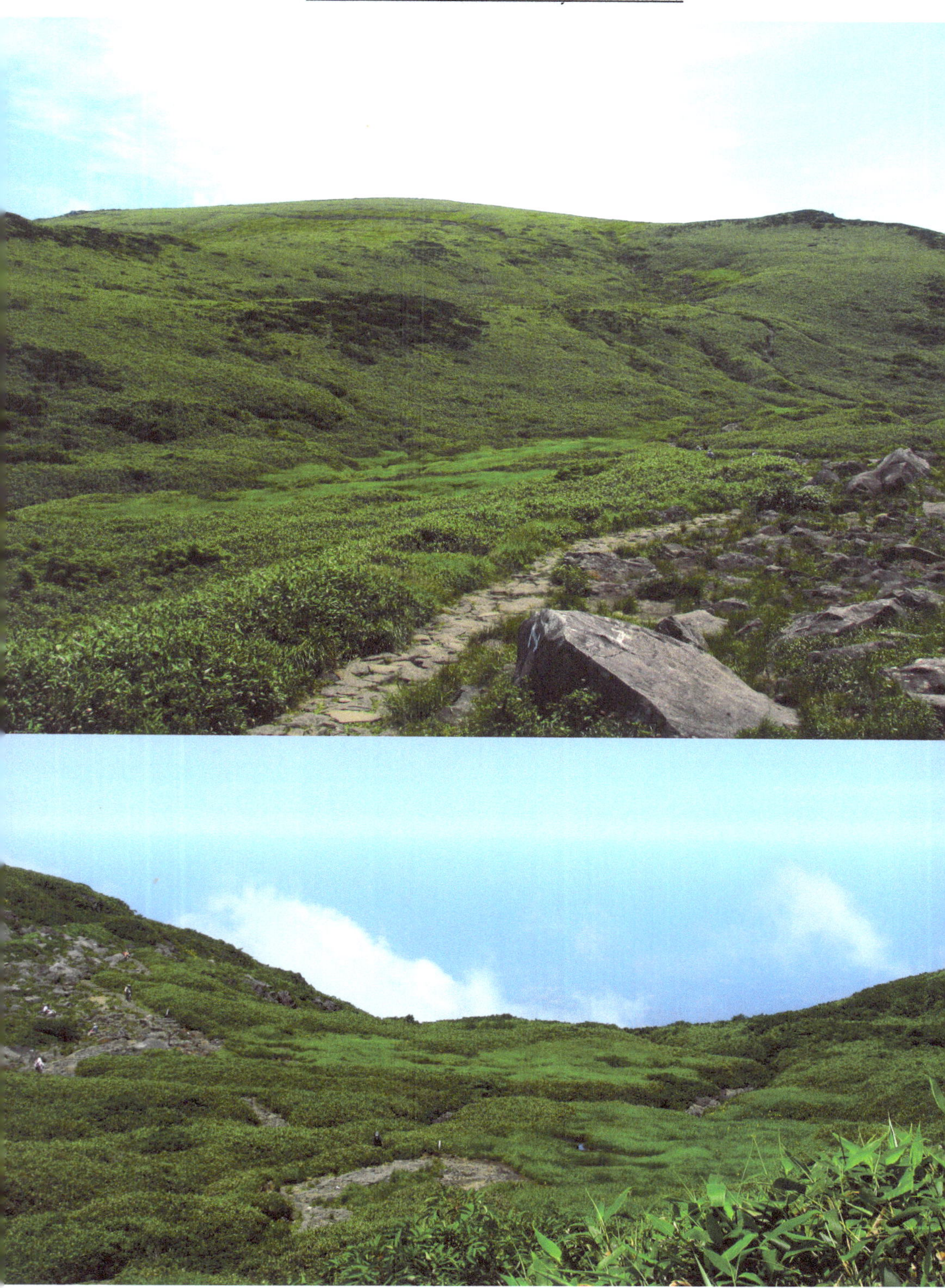

The two photos on the facing page are the final two which we'll show that were taken along the trail before we arrived at the hut just to the north of the "Lake" annotation. In these two photos you can again appreciate the amazing green and in the upper photo you can also see the trail. If you search, you can also see people in both photos.

The next image is a two photo panorama of the small lake which is annotated as "Lake" on the map on page 11. This is actually named Cho-kai Lake. This is a 2005 photo.

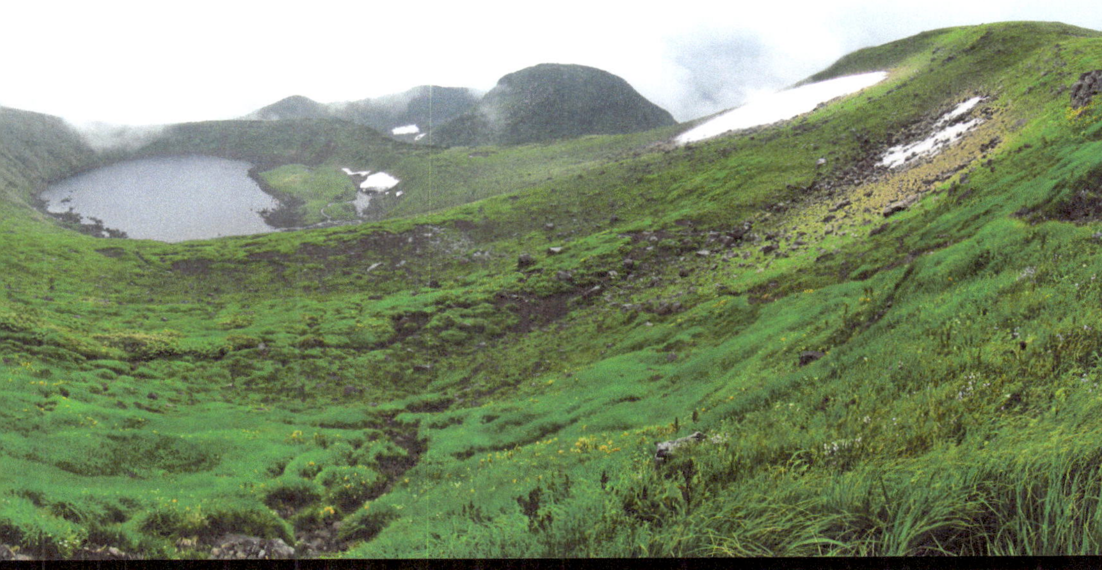

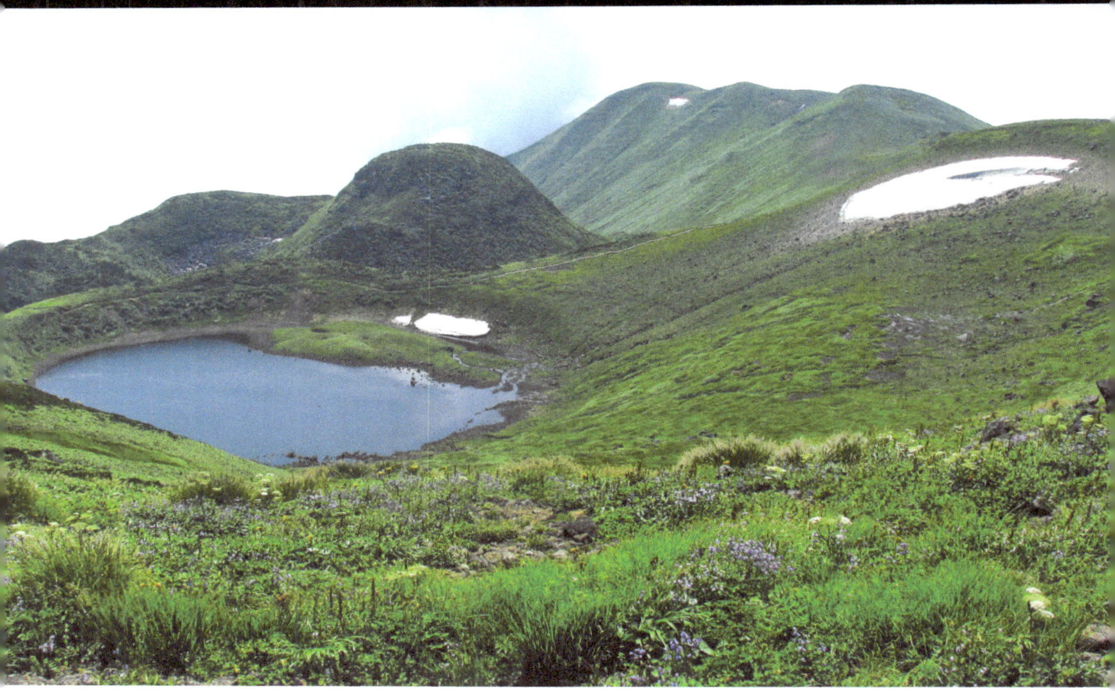

The lower image on the preceding page, also a two photo panorama, is also of Chokai Lake, but it was taken in 2008 and also taken from a different spot.   An interesting thing to note is the snow in both images. When we visited in 2008 we each commented that "it seems like there is less snow than there was back in 2005," but if you study each of these images you can see that it actually appears to be a very similar amount and also in approximately the same places. You will note that the weather was a bit more clear in the 2008 image.

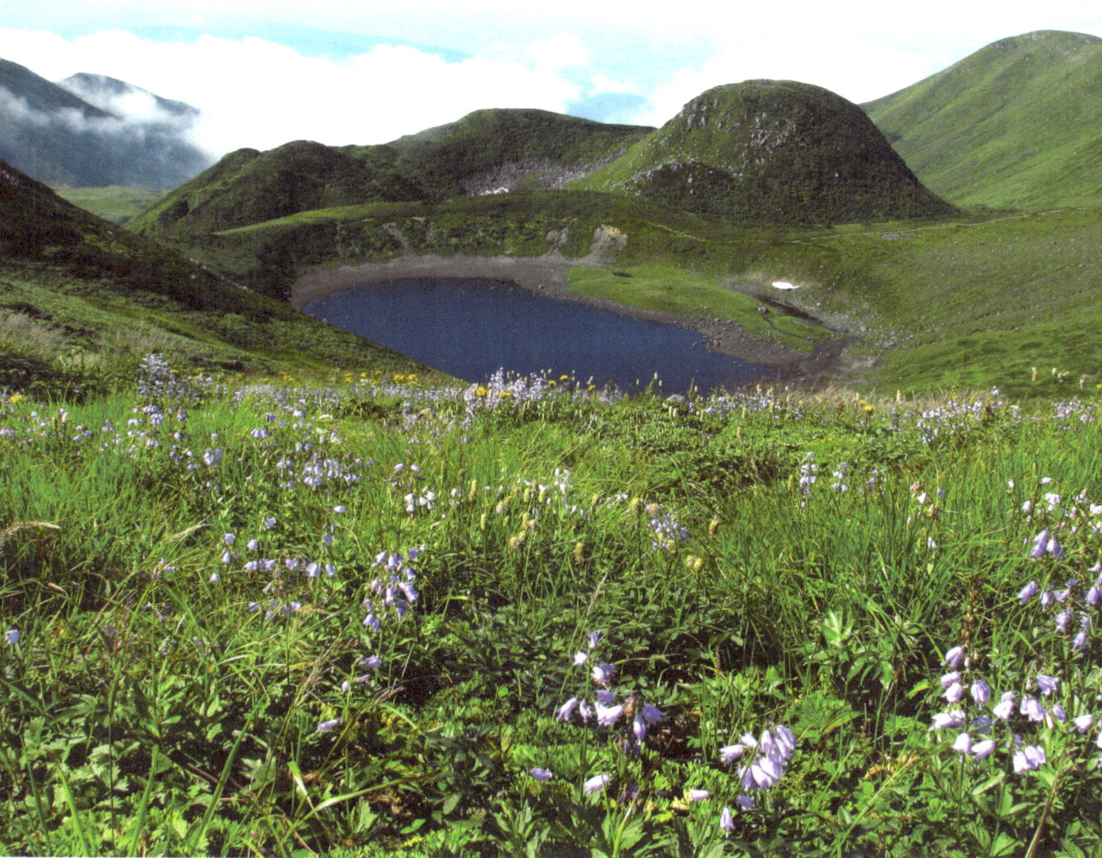

In 2011, when we passed by this area on our ascent it was quite clouded in and we really have no decent photos at all, but the above one was taken during our descent on the following day. It was taken from quite a different place and therefore the angle is also very different, but you'll note that this year there was very little snow left in that spot near the lake where there was a fair amount in both 2005 and in 2008. In this photo please note the abundance of wildflowers.

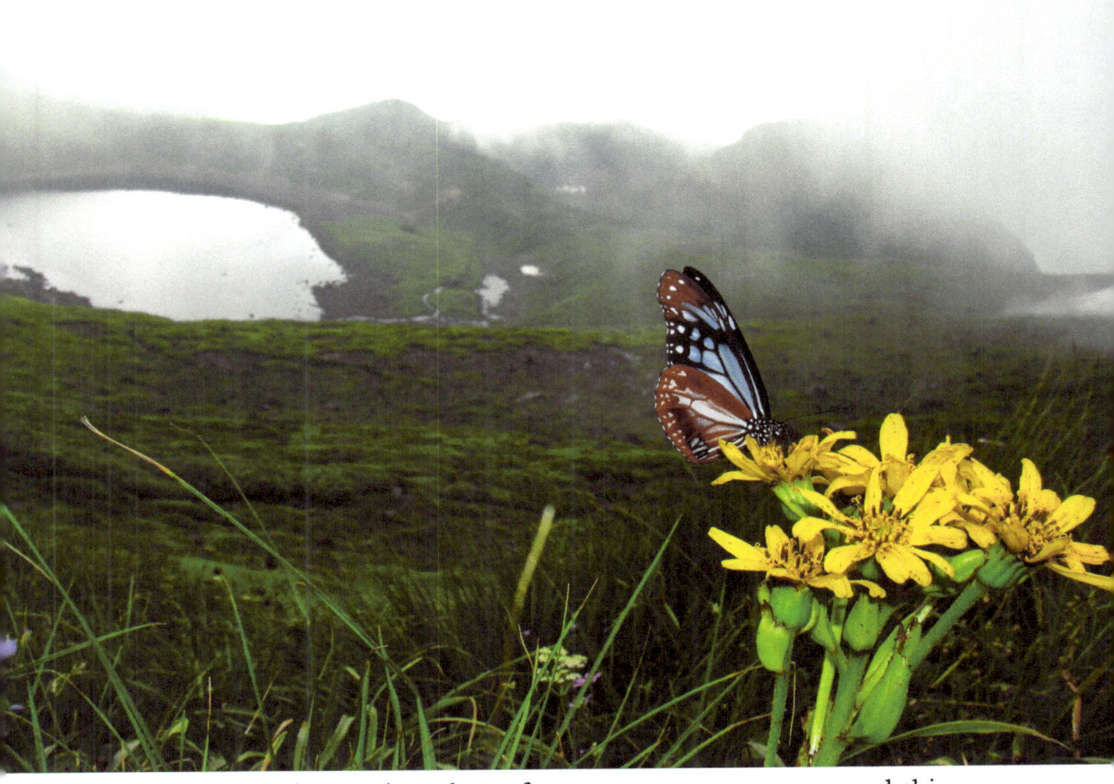

The most interesting photo from our ascent as we passed this area in 2011 is inserted just above. Now you can see what we meant just above when we said it was quite clouded in.

Now, if you don't mind, we'd like to insert some additional photos of this general area which we took during our descent in 2011. In the first image on the following page you can just see the very edge of Chokai Lake, but you can see that snowfield on the mountainside which you could see in the 2005 and 2008 photos (page 15) and it looks like it is of a similar size as it was in both of those years. You'll also note a rope beside the trail. What is its purpose? Is it to help people navigate the trail in whiteout conditions, or is it to keep people from wandering around and trampling on the flowers, which are very abundant here? There are even Edelweiss plants and flowers (*Leontopodium* sp.) very close to this spot.

The second photo on the following page is zoomed in to that small rounded mountain named Mt. Nabemori (1,652 m = 5,420 ft). Wonder how many people bother with climbing to its summit? Probably not very many, but to us it looks interesting. In that photo you can also see the trail which passes between Chokai Lake and Mt. Nabemori.

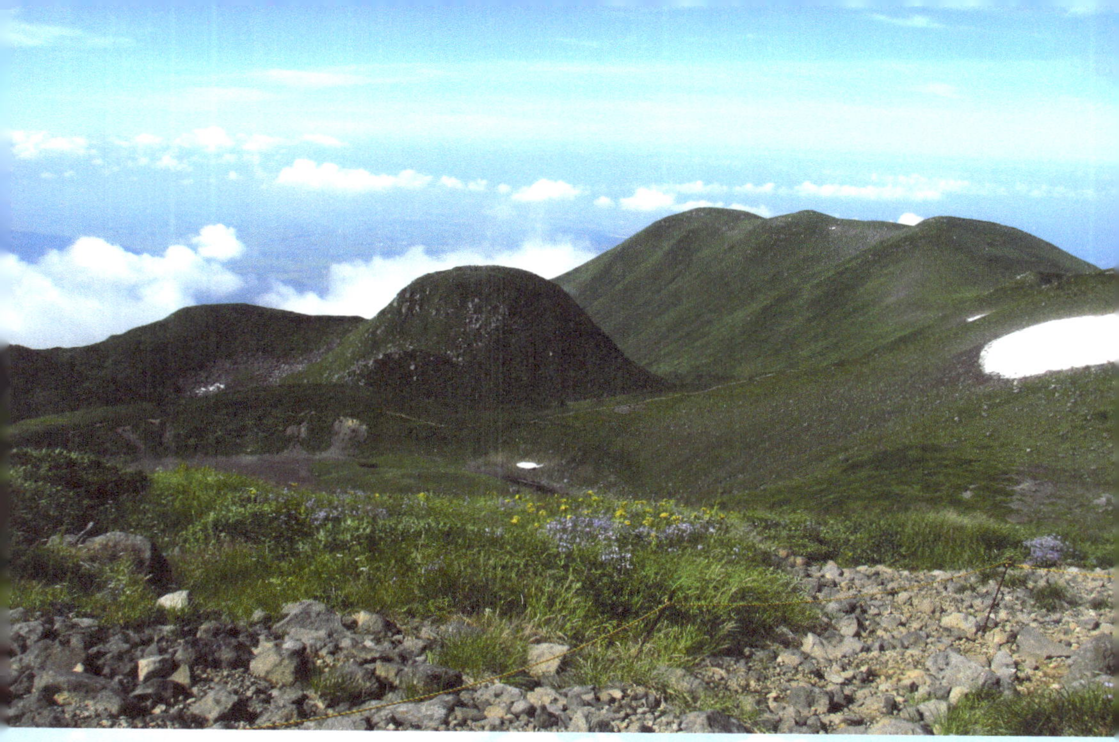

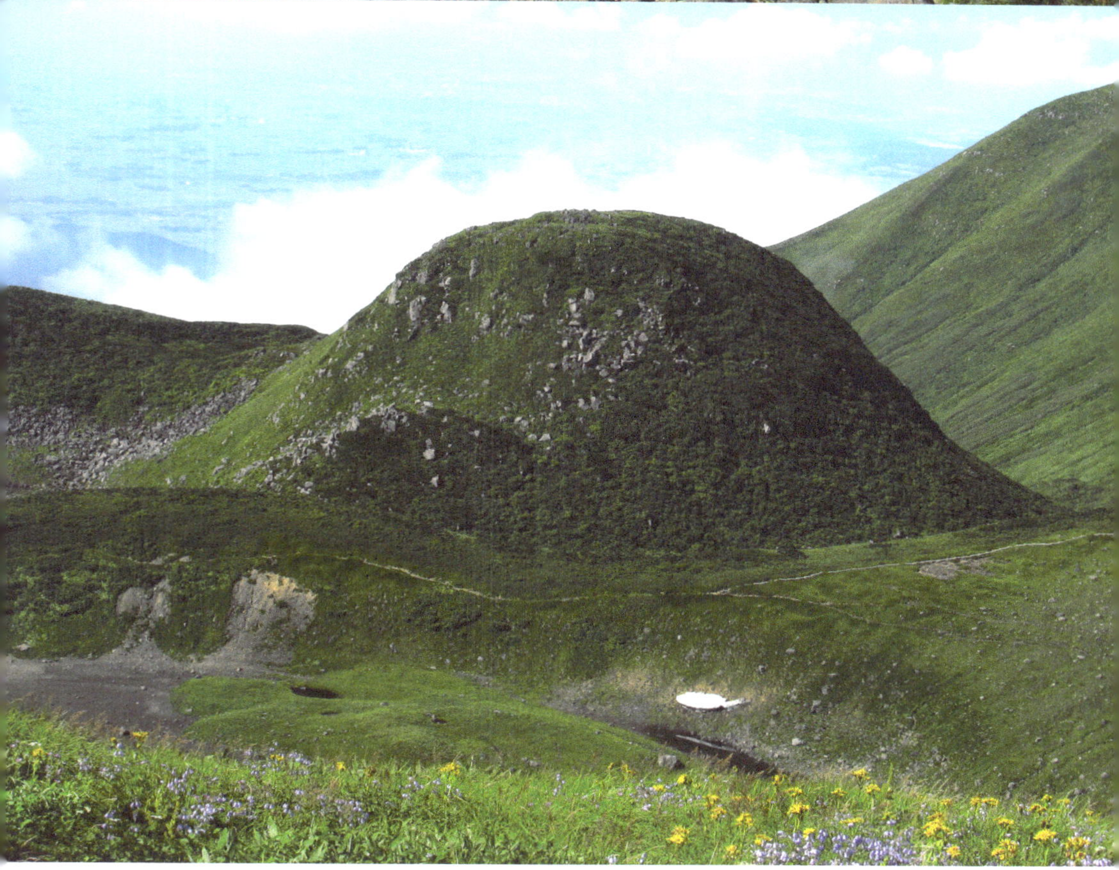

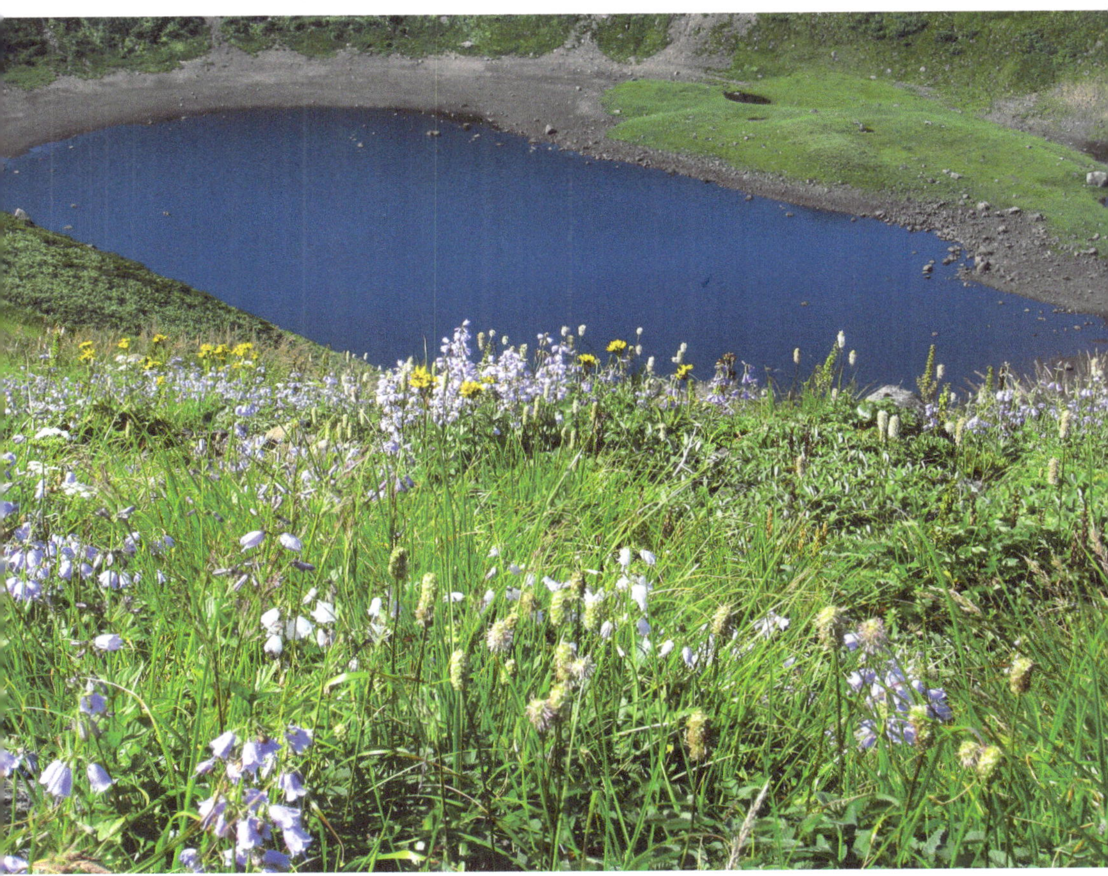

The photo immediately above is one which is zoomed in to show pretty much only Chokai Lake and the wildflowers growing between here and the lake. This photo was taken in 2011 as we descended the mountain. The spot it was taken from was quite close to the panoramic view mark (✱) on the map between the 1. and 2. annotations.

On the following page are two additional shots taken in 2011 from near this spot. The upper one shows me hiking along between the 1. and 2. annotations on the map, and in this photo you can see the hut which is just north of Chokai Lake. In the distance you can also see the Sea of Japan.

The lower photo on the next page is nearly the final shot you will see which shows Chokai Lake. This photo is beautiful both for the amazing greens and also for the great abundance of wildflowers. You should also notice that Mt. Nabemori is on the right edge of this photo.

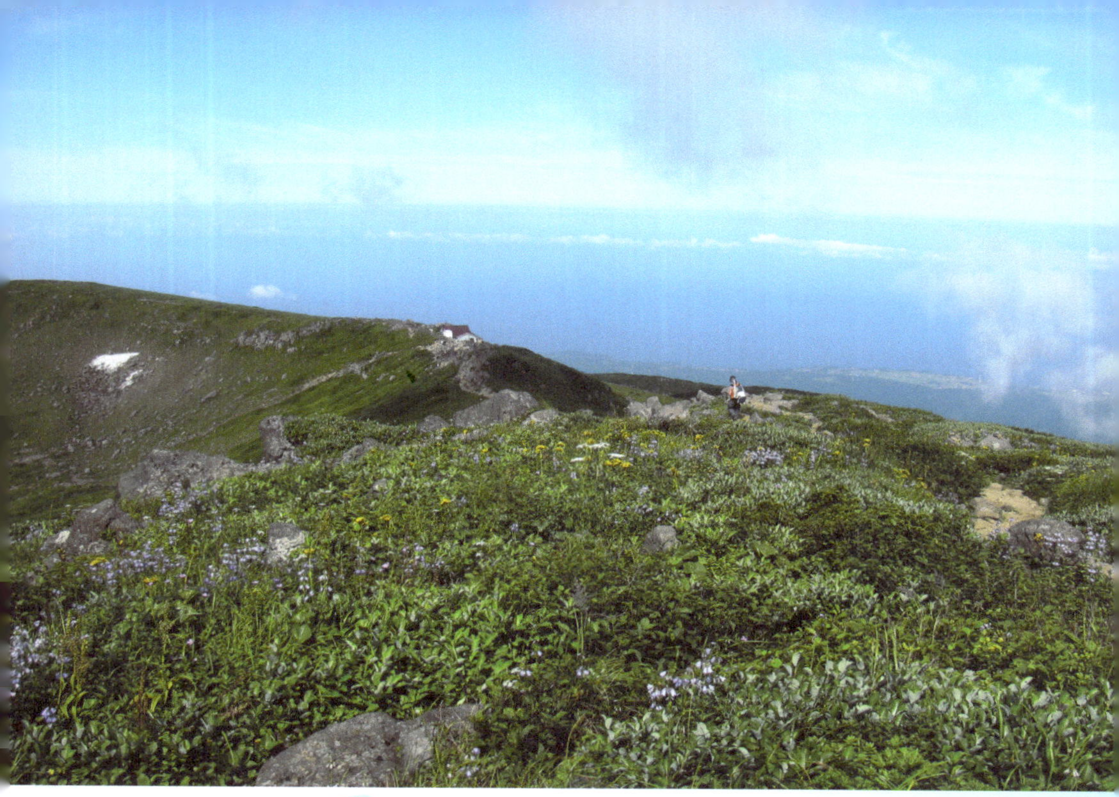

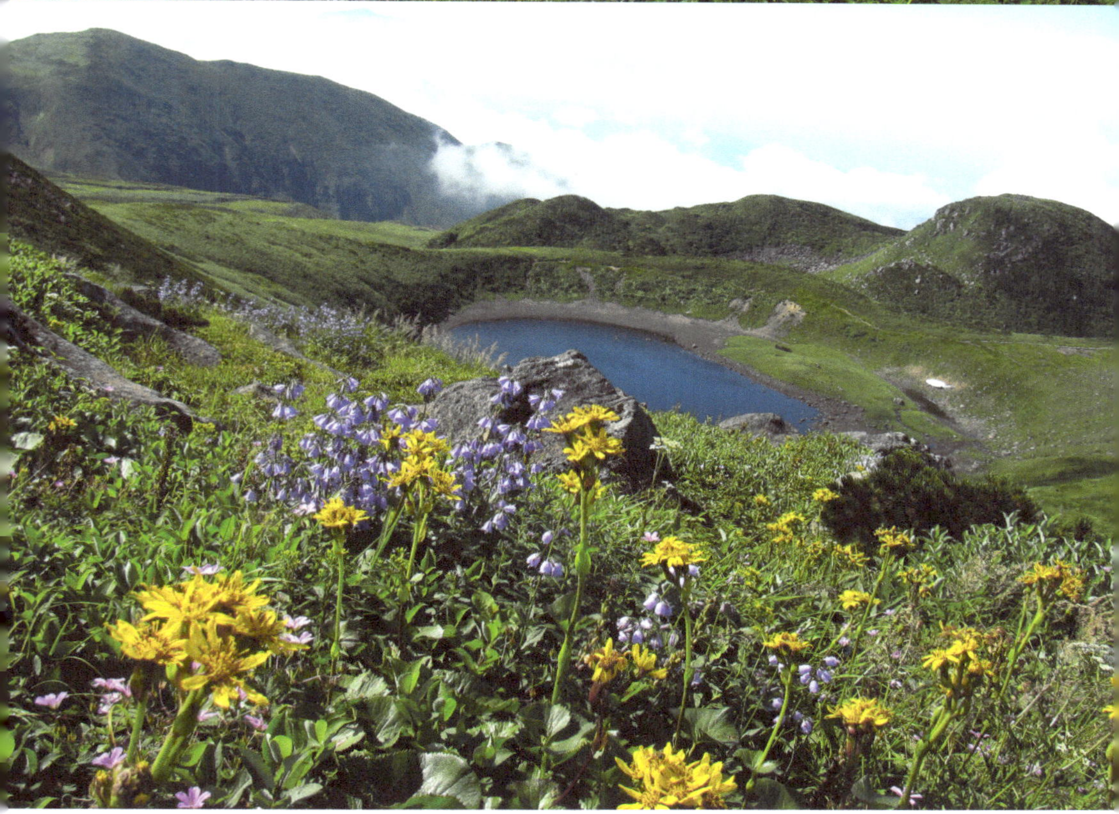

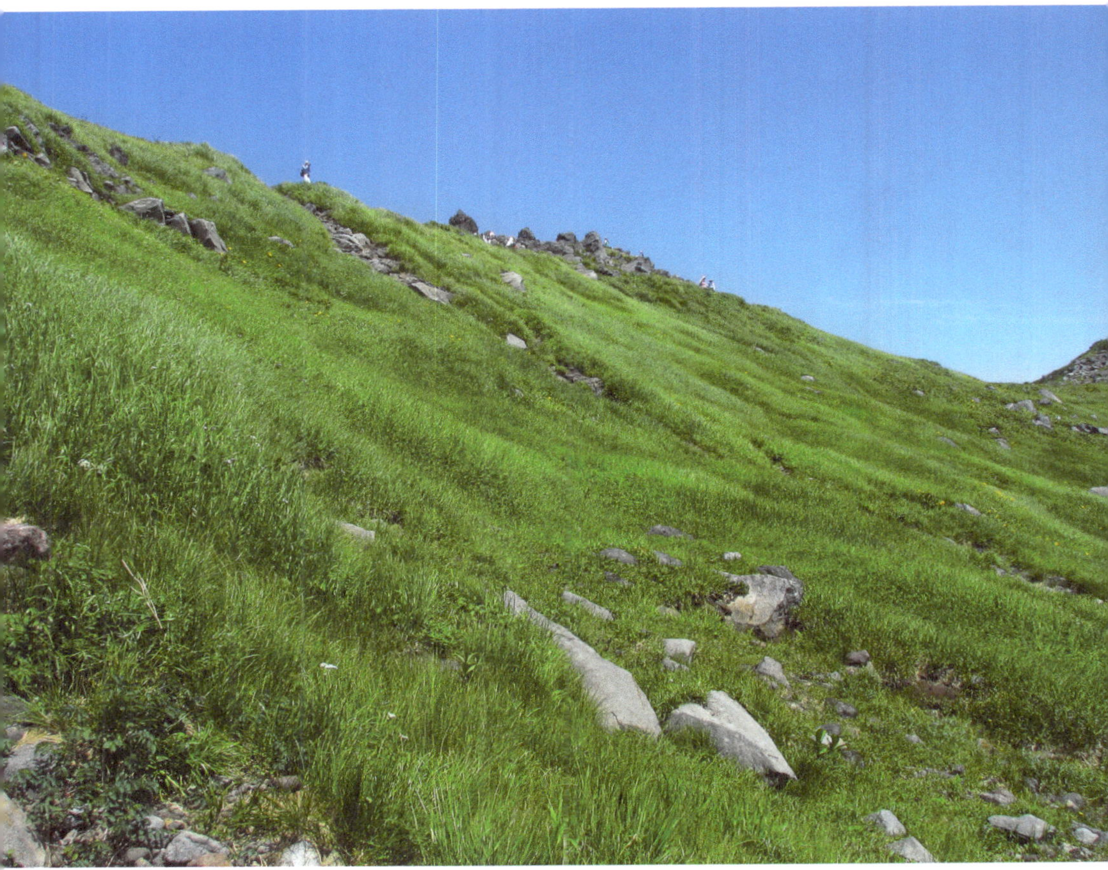

Now, how about two or three photos taken during our 2008 climb which show the "wall" of the crater of Chokai Lake? The first one, just above, shows that there is not much growing right here except for grasses. You can see people up there at the top, too. The hut would be just to the left of this photo by approximately 200 meters.

The second photo, shown on the next page, shows you that there are a great deal of rocks here. In this photo, near the upper right corner, you can see one side of one of the hut buildings. The person standing near the center of the photo is Kazuya.

In the third photo, also on the following page, you can see the summit area of Mt. Chokai near the upper right corner. You can also see people in this photo, up on the green ridge above us, but they are merely black specks that stick up above the vegetation. This should give you an idea of the scale of things – in other words, this is a huge green area with an abundance of rocks.

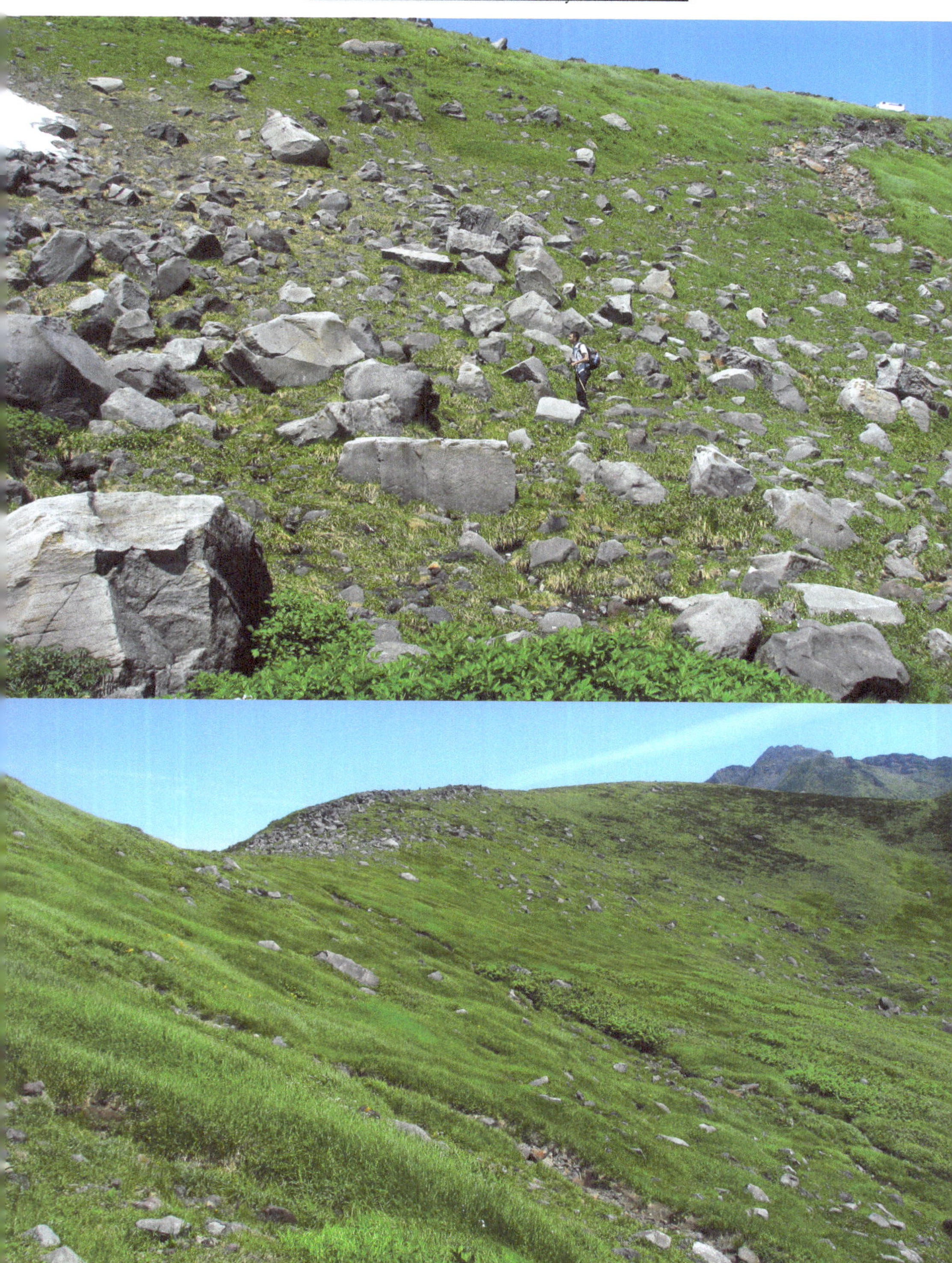

Okay, now let's proceed from this area and get ourselves into gear for the remainder of the climb up to the summit. The easy part is behind us, but the more difficult parts are still ahead of us. Around this first hut area, though, is a great place to take a lunch break and if the weather is fine, to do a bunch of photography of both flowers and also scenery. It's extremely easy to spend an hour or more in this area. You can also get a cup of coffee here at the hut.

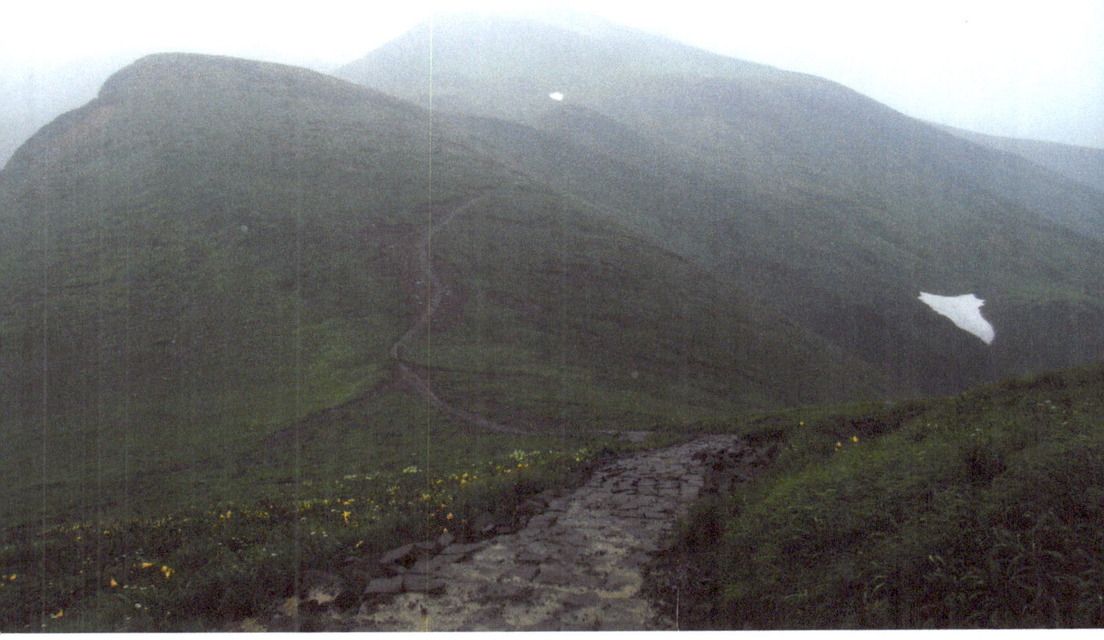

The photo immediately above was taken as we climbed in 2005. It had started to rain while we were eating our lunch near the hut to the north of Chokai Lake. It was taken at 12:56 PM along the trail between the 1. and 2. annotations on the map. Off in the distance there, near the center of the photo, is the summit area, but the actual summit is hidden in the clouds. The distances here are very deceiving to the eye. You can see the trail snaking its way down this hill we are on and across that valley or pass ahead of us and then going up the side of the slope ahead – it's going to take a while to arrive at the final spot we can see in this photo.

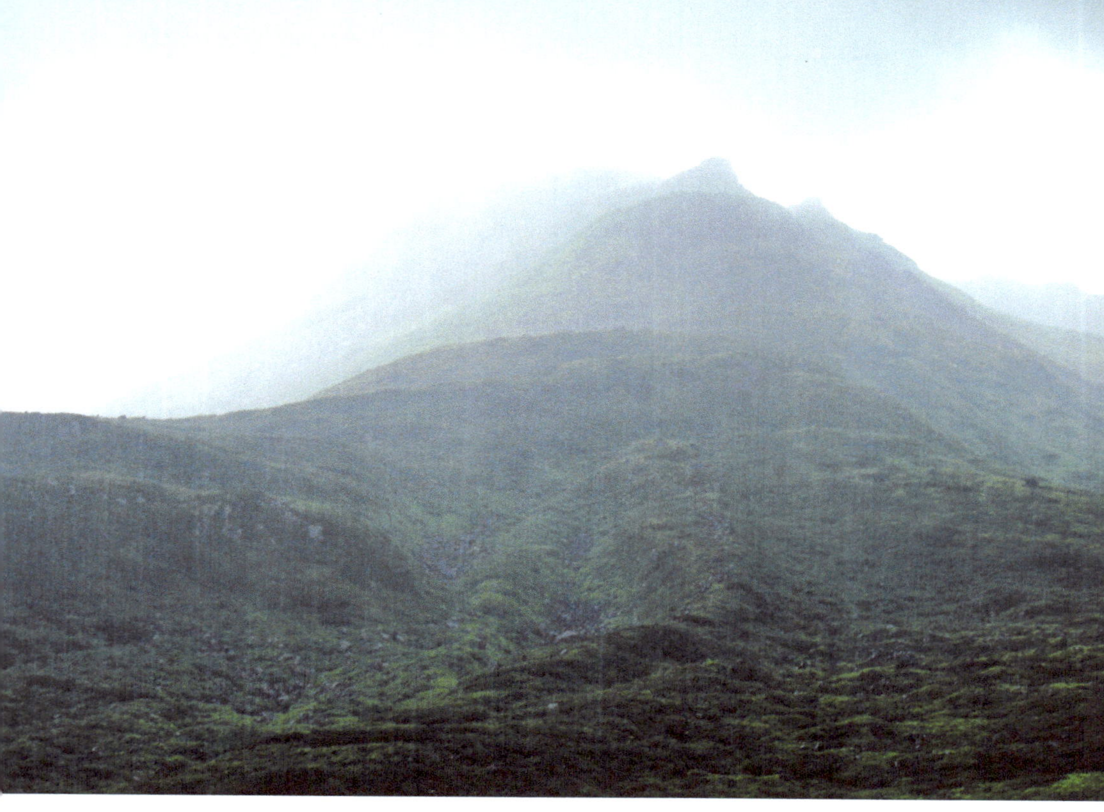

This photo just above was taken on the same date in 2005 and just about exactly one hour later – at 1:52 PM. This photo has been processed so that you can actually see the rain falling in it – that is what those vertical streaks are, the rain falling. The summit is nearly visible in this photo, it is the area just to the left of the center of the photo. We were actually shooting these photos from under umbrellas. You may say "umbrellas, you took umbrellas with you, how could you afford the weight?" Well, when you stay in the hut for the night that means that you don't need to carry along a sleeping bag or a tent. In addition, you have a choice of being able to eat the meals provided by the hut or bring your own food. We have always taken our own food when we have climbed this mountain, as the food provided by the summit hut is not very nice looking. We have always taken the fixings for sandwiches, some protein bars and some high energy foods, and that means we also did not need to carry along a cook stove or gas. So, umbrellas were not really a burden as far as additional weight.

The following photo (facing page) was taken in 2008, at about noon as we ascended from the Chokai Lake area, what beautiful weather, eh? The summit of the mountain is just a tiny bit to the left of center. It appears that we still have a long way to go, and that is correct.

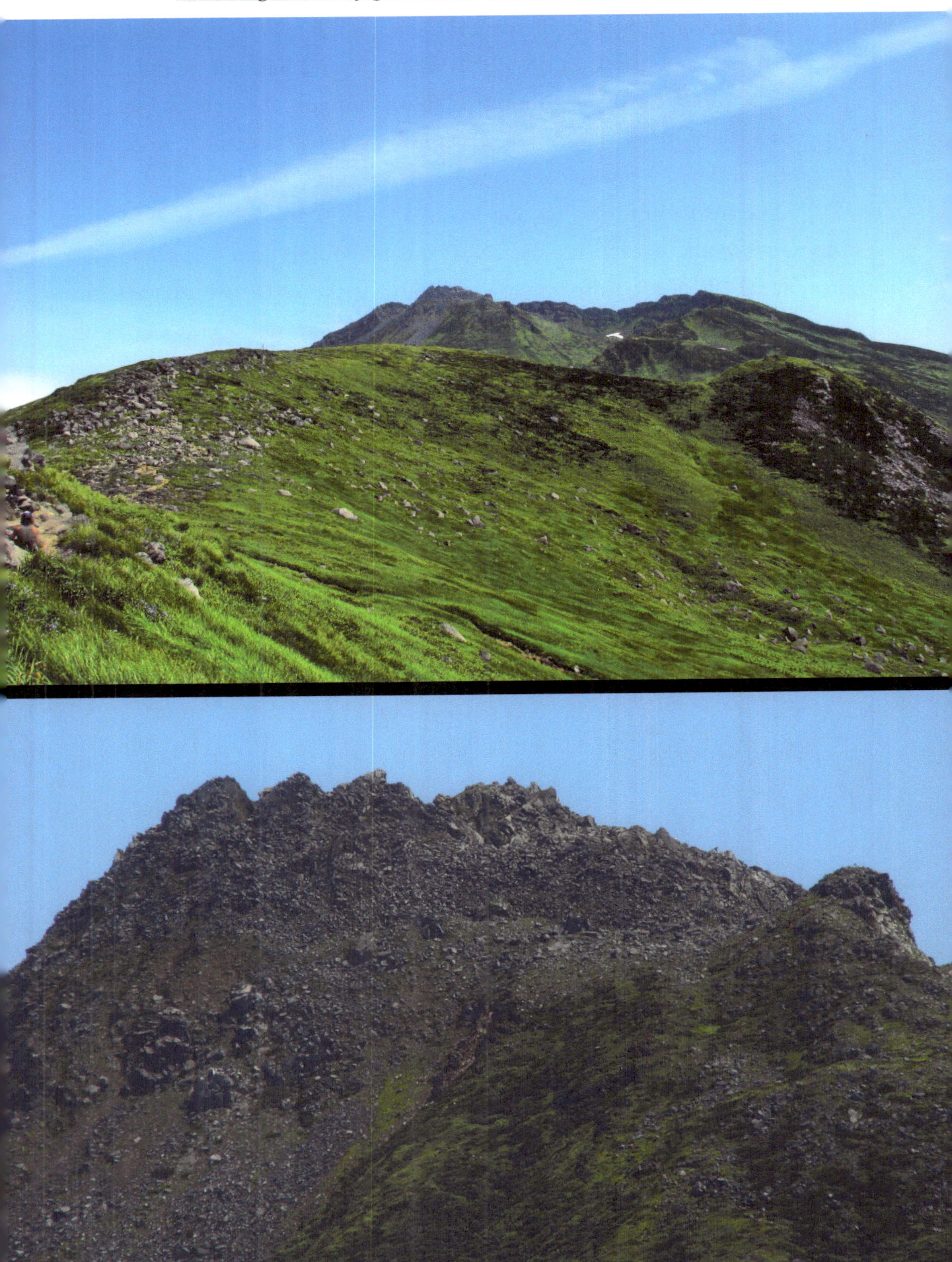

The lower photo on the preceding page was taken from just about precisely the same place as the photo above it, and just one minute later, but it is zoomed in to the summit of the mountain. As you can see, the summit is very rocky – and just wait until we show you some photos of the summit when we get closer to it, you'll see that – yes, it's rocky!

The next photo is also one from 2008, and was taken from a spot very close to the photo on page 23. It was taken one hour and eight minutes (at 1:14 PM) after the preceding photo. It shows the summit and the large horseshoe shaped area to the right of the summit. You can easily see the trail and several people in this photo.

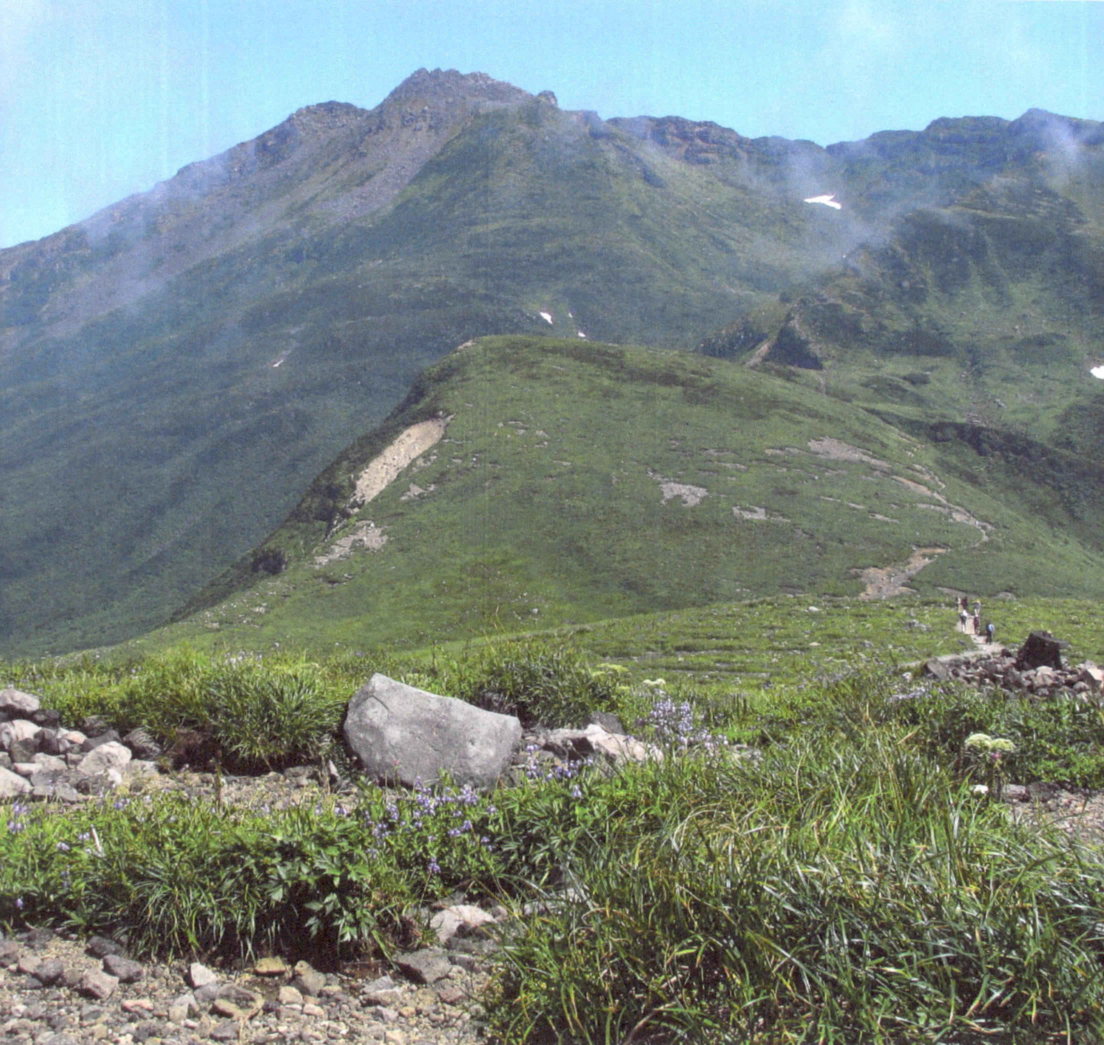

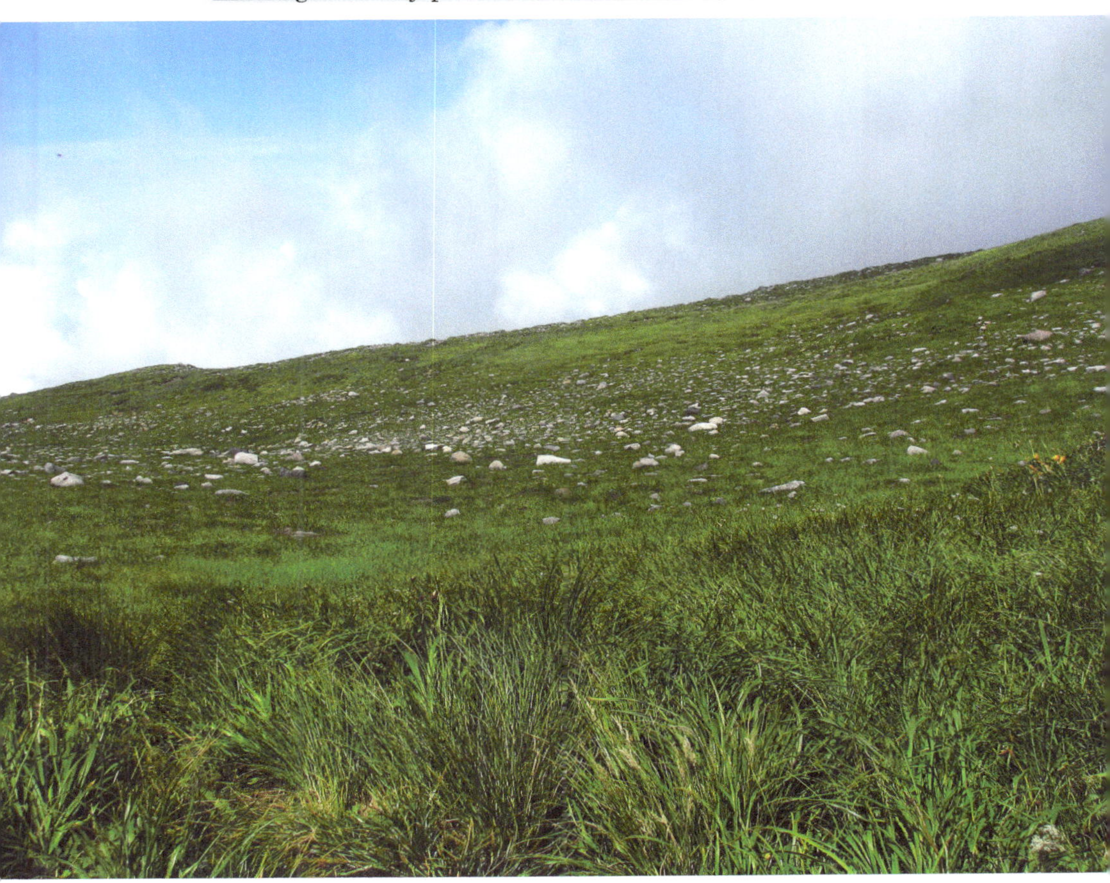

The photo immediately above was taken about twenty minutes after the one on the facing page and was taken on that large green hillside which you can see directly in front of us. It was included herein to show you the beautiful greens and also so that you can appreciate how rocky and relatively barren this area is. There is a lot of grass and there are also many small alpine flowers, but nothing of any height at all, not even a bush of any kind.

The next photo (following page) was taken at nearly 2:00 PM on the same date in 2008, the weather is still absolutely beautiful and we do not have a care or complaint of any kind. The location is at the trail junction just past the 2. annotation on the map (page 11). You can see both of the trails in this photo – or at least you can see people on the hillside above the cliff, as well as people below the cliff. We will climb via the lower trail – the one below the cliff. When we descend we will come via the upper trail. You will also note that you can see the summit of Mt. Chokai to the left of center – and it still looks a long ways ahead.

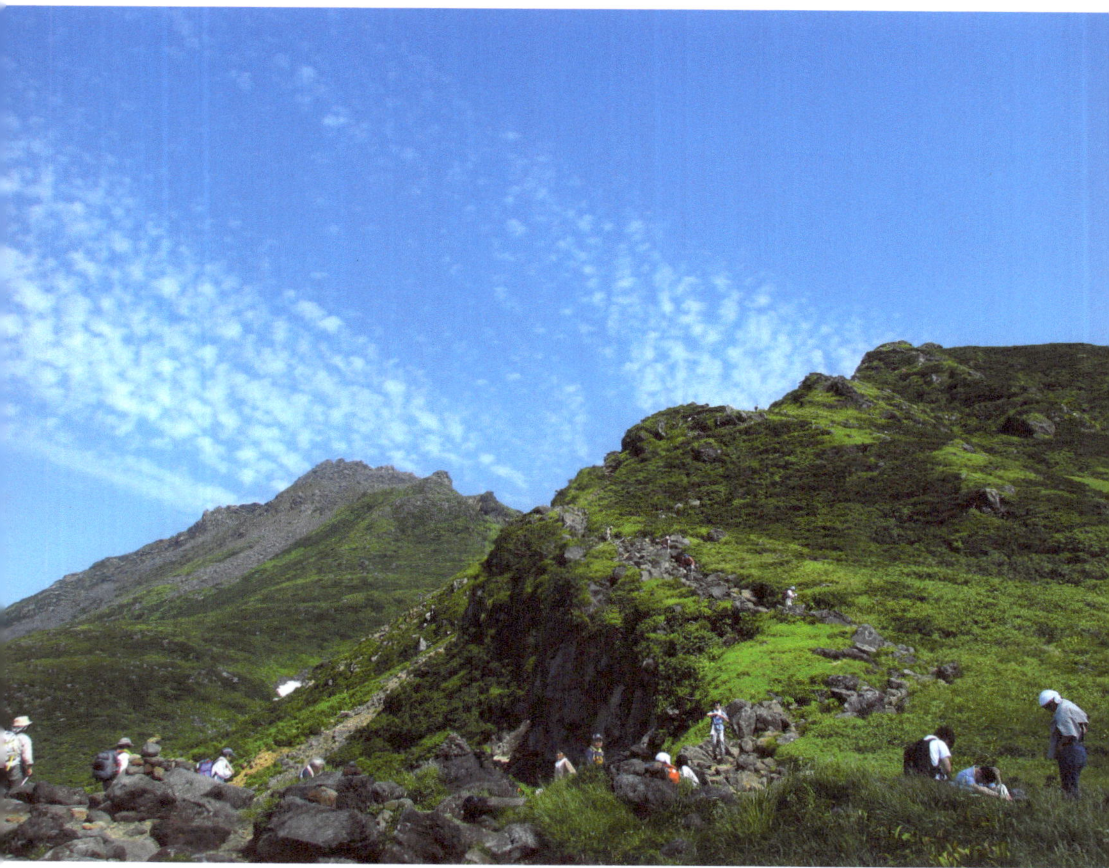

Now there are no photos for a while. There are several dangerous places on the trail we followed and that fact is so indicated on the map by this Japanese kanji 危 inside of a circle. When Kazuya and I are hiking or climbing on dangerous places that scare us we seldom take any photos. We are too concerned about climbing the rickety steel ladders which they attach rather precariously to the nearly vertical rock walls and we just try to use our common sense, maintain our footing and be safe.

For this reason there are no additional photos from any of our climbs of this mountain for about the next fifteen or twenty minutes — not until we get beyond the most dangerous area.

The photo on the facing page was taken at 2:14 PM in 2008 — it was our first incredible sight after we had safely passed beyond the most dangerous area. The summit of Mt. Chokai would be to the left of this photo. This shows some amazing green colors and a very large snowfield here on August 9th. You can even see some people on the snowfield so that you can gauge its size quite easily.

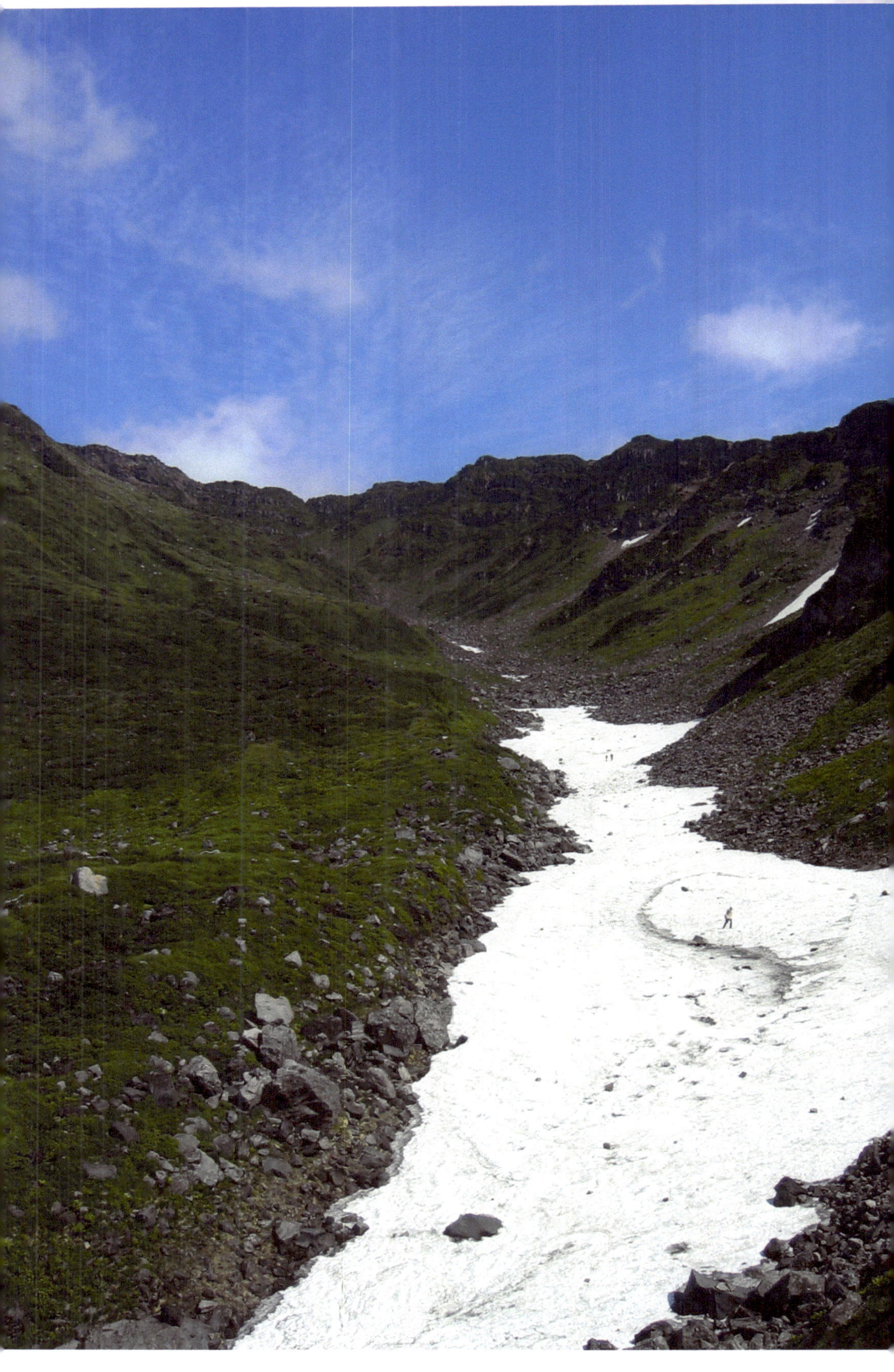

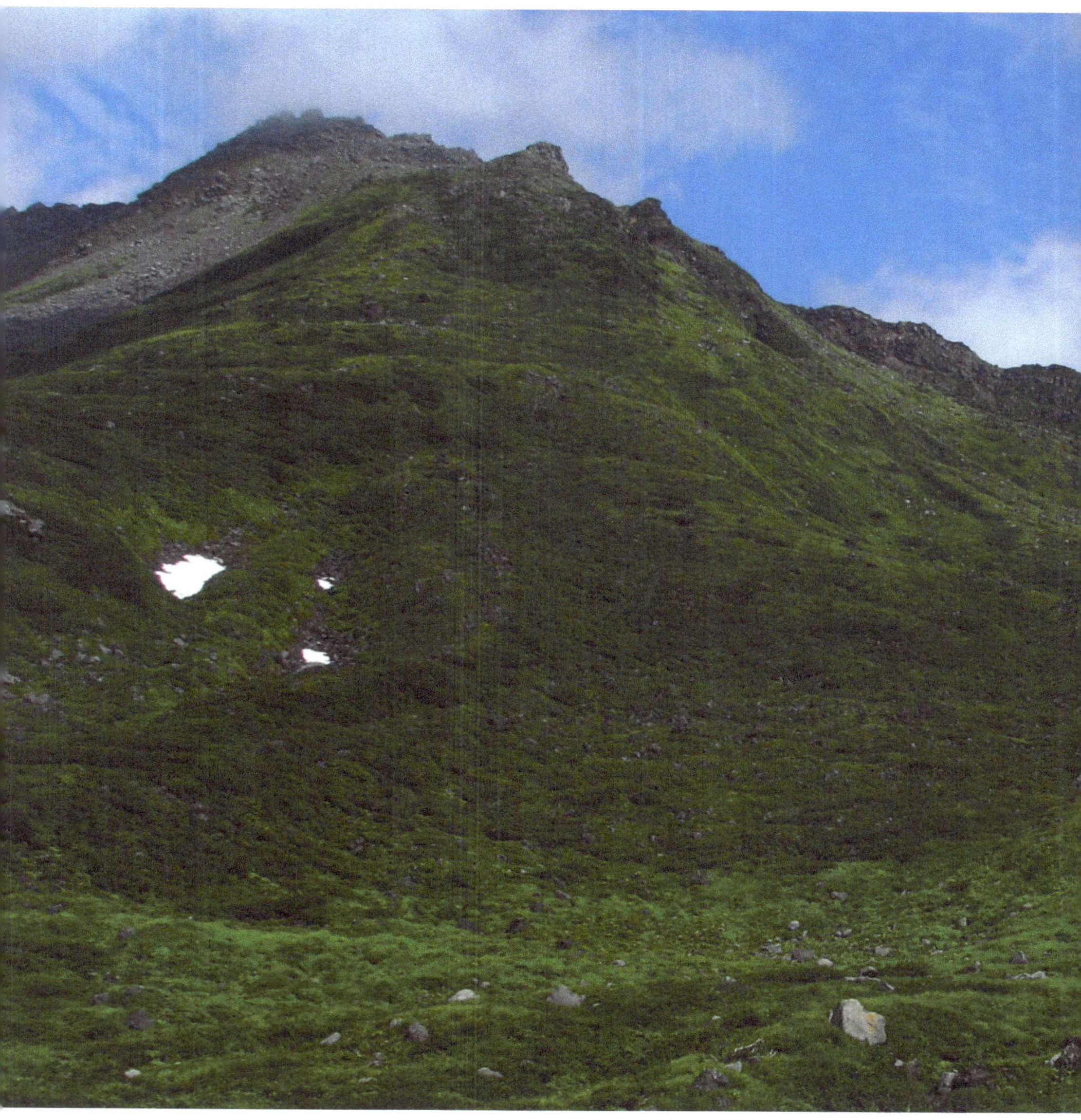

The two-page spread photo, shown above left and above right is a two shot panorama in which you can see both the summit of Mt. Chokai and also the snowfield. It also was taken in 2008, and the weather was so very cooperative on this climb for allowing us to capture some really great photos.

The upper photo on page 32, also taken in 2008, was taken just before we finished crossing the snowfield and shows the summit of Mt. Chokai very beautifully. From this angle it is not possible to see the very summit – it is hidden behind all of the false summits. It is also not pos-

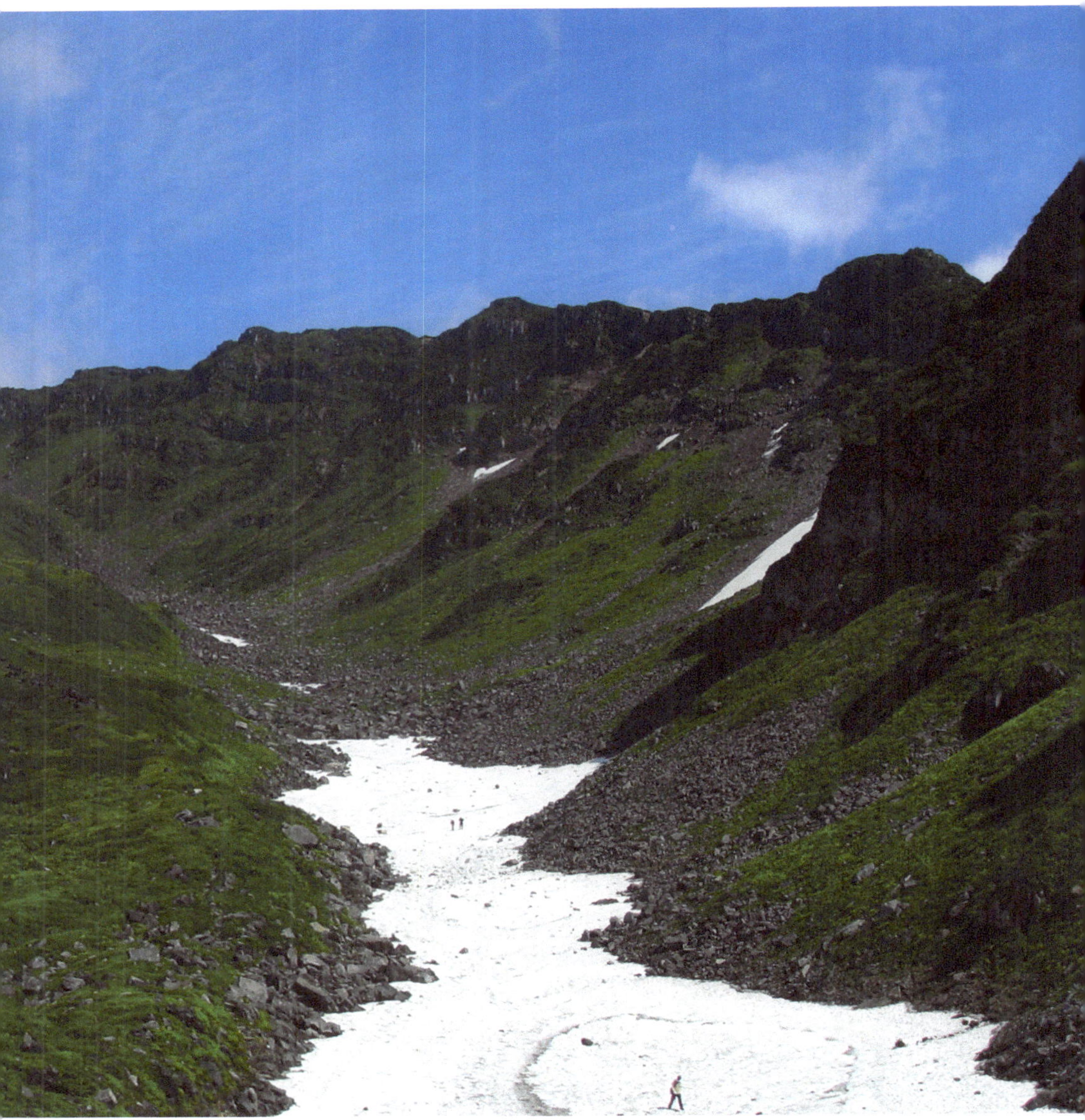

sible to see the location of the hut where we will stay from this angle; one cannot see it until one is virtually on the front steps. One might say that it is very well hidden.

The lower photo on the following page gives you an idea of what the weather was like in this area when we climbed this mountain in 2011. It was not as wonderful as one might have wished for, but at least it was not raining. In this photo you can see the trail on the far side of the snowfield if you study it closely. You can also find at least one person on the trail if you study it even more closely.

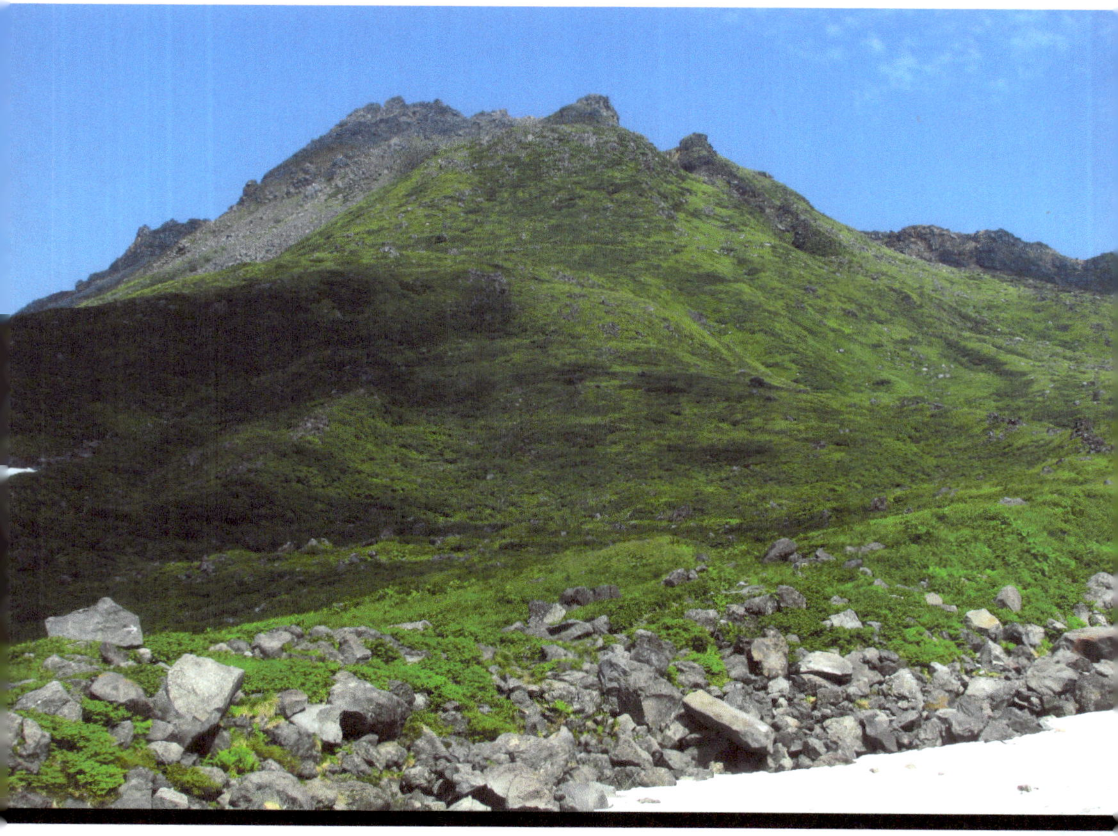

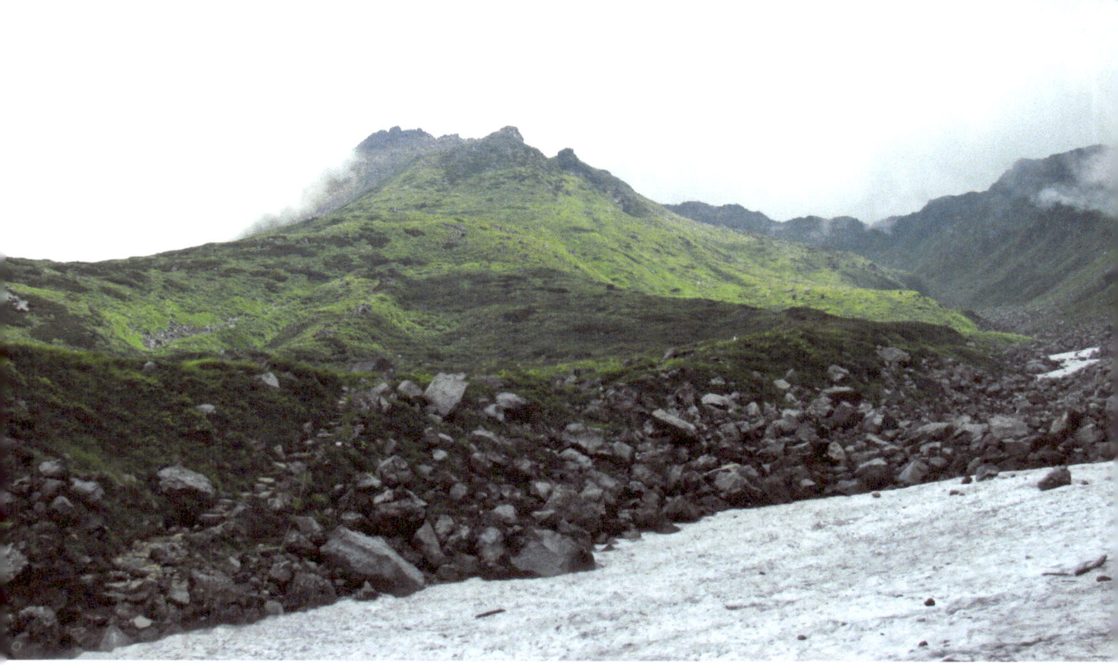

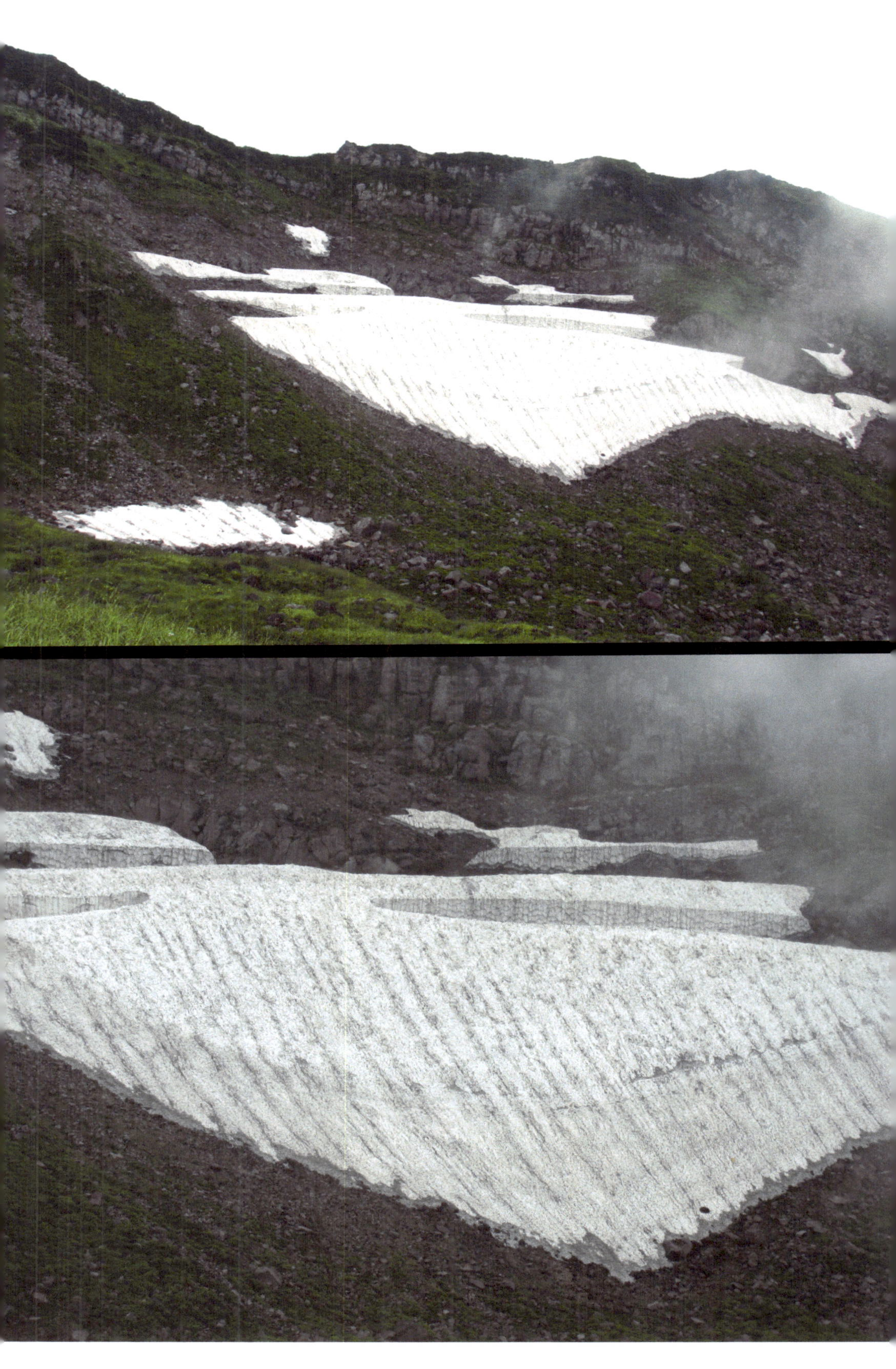

The upper photo on the previous page is interesting. It was taken in 2011 after we had passed by the snowfield shown in the photos on pages 29, 31 and 32 and it shows a strangely melted out snowdrift which was on the right side of the valley which you can see in the lower photo on page 32. The lower photo on the previous page shows the same snowdrift, but this photo is zoomed in so that the strange melt pattern can be seen more closely. You can see that it has melted so that some nearly perfectly vertical walls have been created as it melted away. Our question is – why and how did this happen? You should also remember that the date is August 8. It looks like there is still quite a bit of snow remaining in this drift, it's quite obviously not going to totally disappear before the new snow starts falling.

There are no more photos between here and the hut which we would like to show you. So, the next photo shows you the hut area. It was taken at 5:56 PM on August 11, 2005 as we scrambled our way to the summit from the hut.

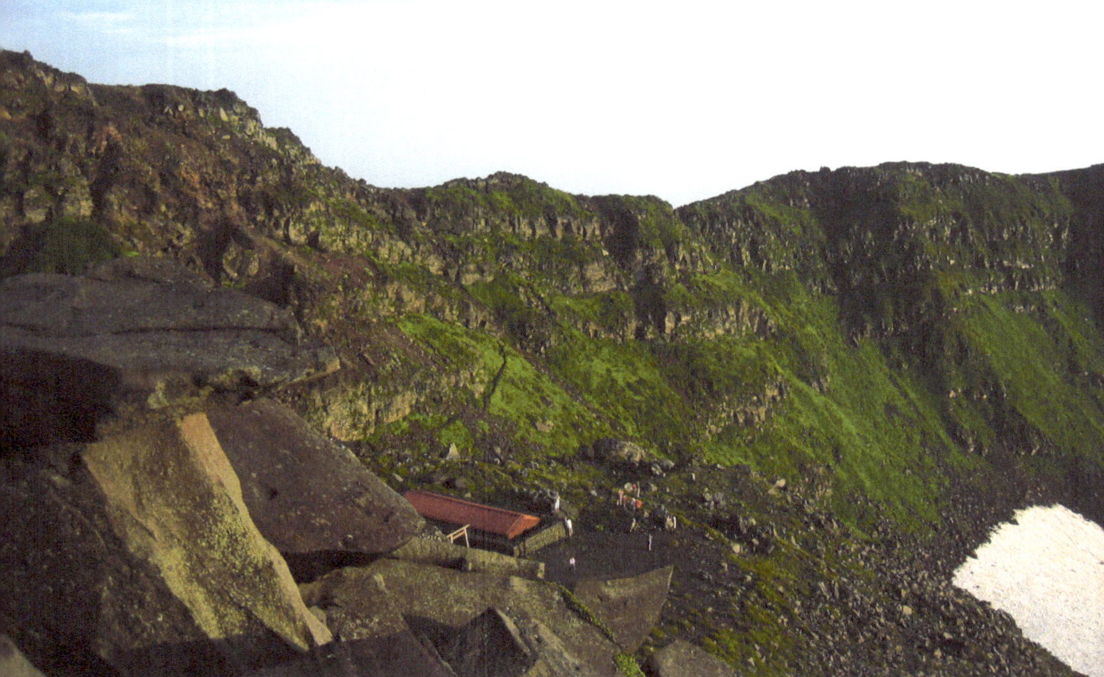

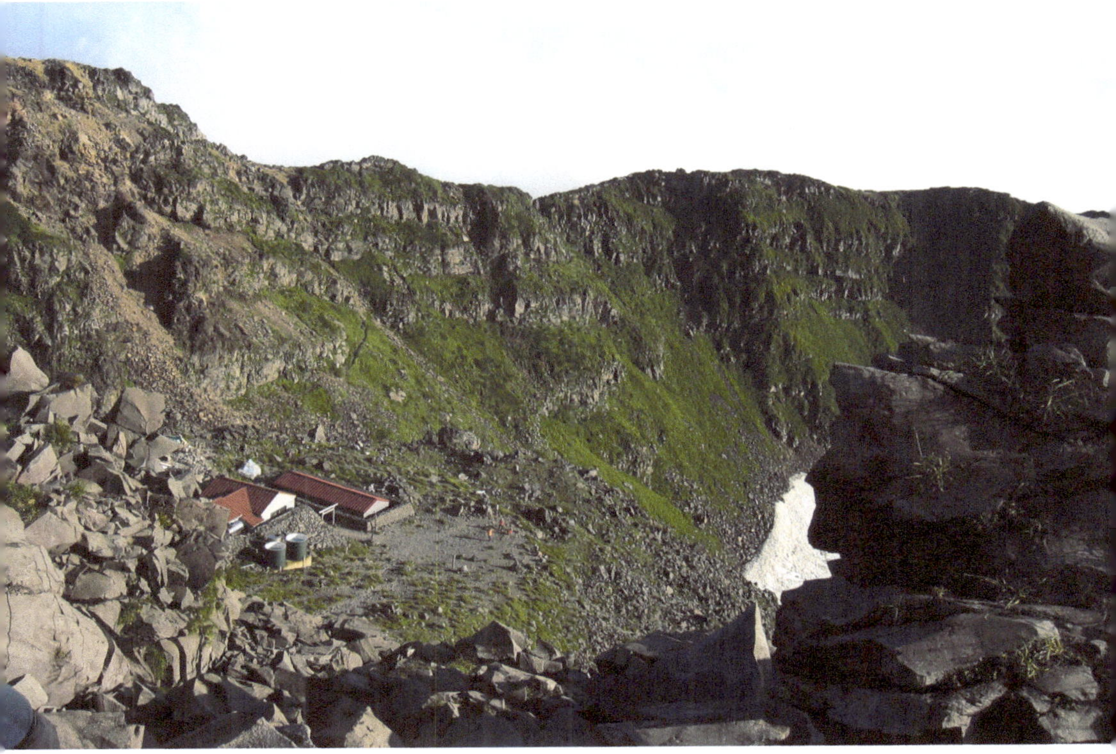

The photo just above was taken at 5:00 PM on August 9, 2008. It also shows the hut area as we scrambled our way to the summit. It is different enough from the 2005 photo so that we wanted to show it to you.

Now, we'll show you precisely what we were scrambling around and over. The photo just below shows this extremely rocky slope which we are scrambling up as we strive for the summit.

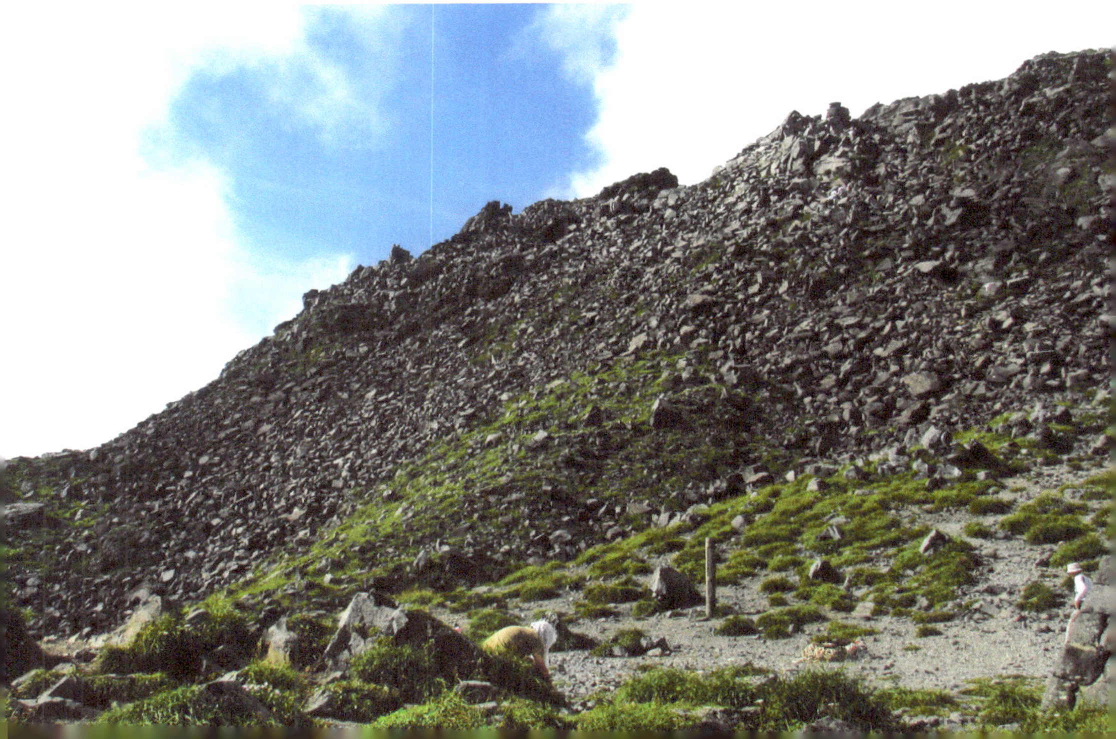

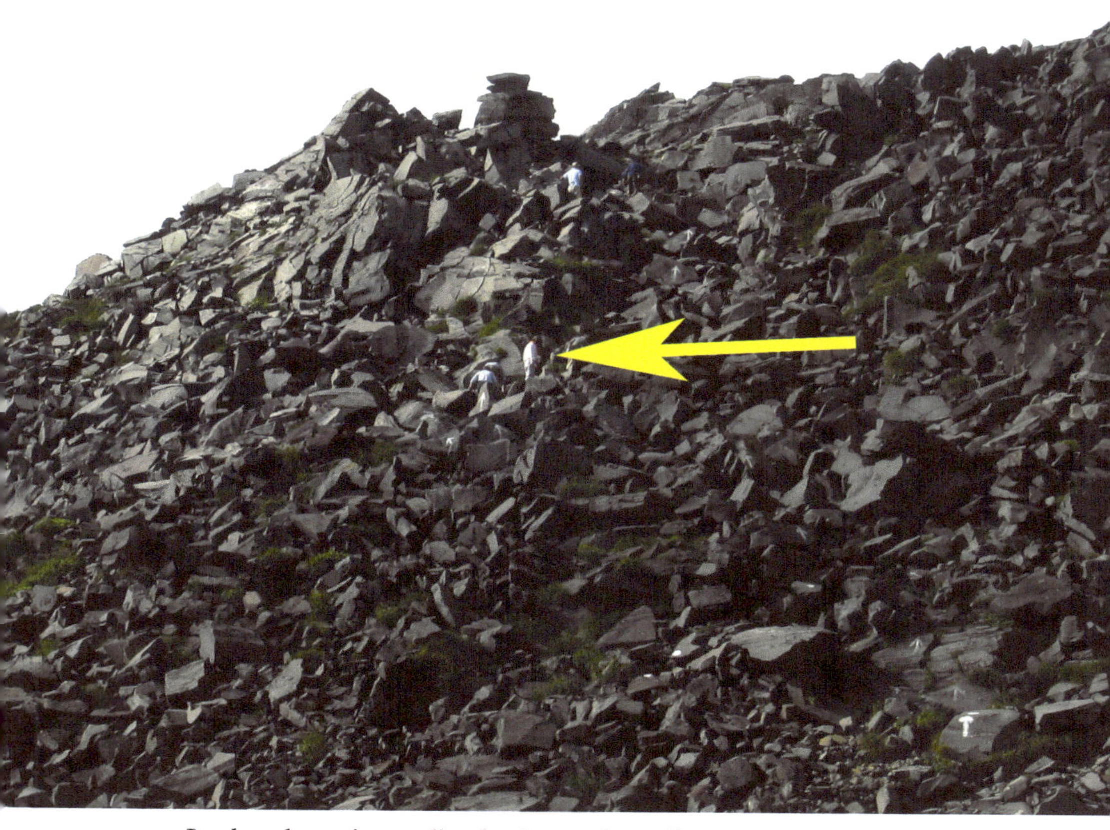

In the photo immediately above the yellow arrow points to a person, so you can get a feel for the scale of everything and also the size of these huge boulders.

The photo on the facing page has no people in it for scale, but we are going to go between those rock walls which you can see ahead. The photo on page 38 shows me going between these rocky walls so that you have something for scale, but that photo was taken from somewhere ahead of where the facing page photo was taken and we wanted to show you the next photo just to kind of confuse you as to the scale of every-thing. You will note the white arrows on the rocks, indicating which way we should proceed. Both of these photos (facing page and on page 38) were taken on August 8, 2011 at around 5:30 PM.

The first time we climbed this mountain, in 2005, we were not paying close enough attention to the white arrows, or maybe they were not so prominent back in 2005, but for whatever reason, on our first attempt to get to the summit we did not make it – we ended up on one of the many false summits which you can end up on if you are not careful to search for and follow the arrows which point the way.

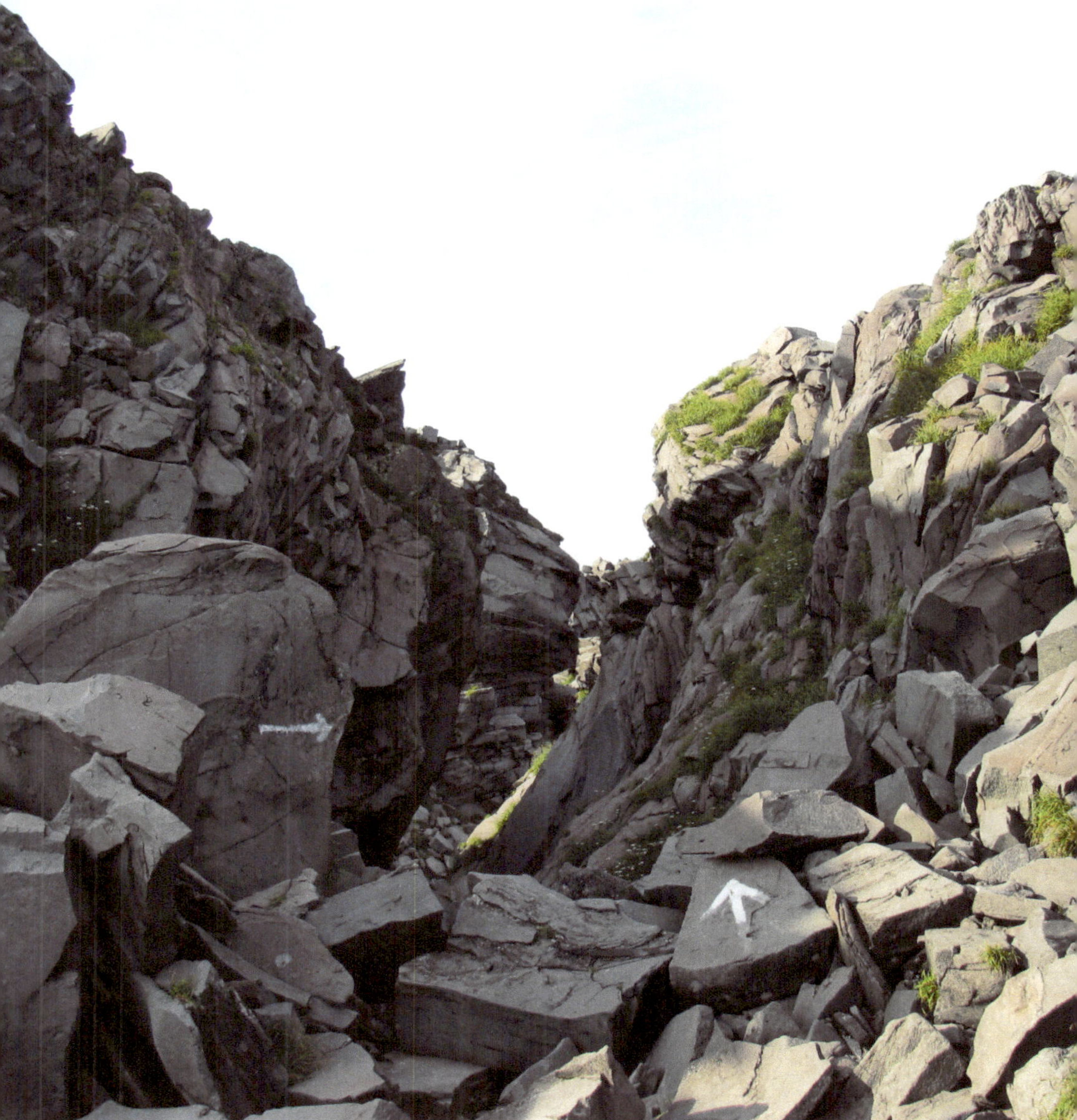

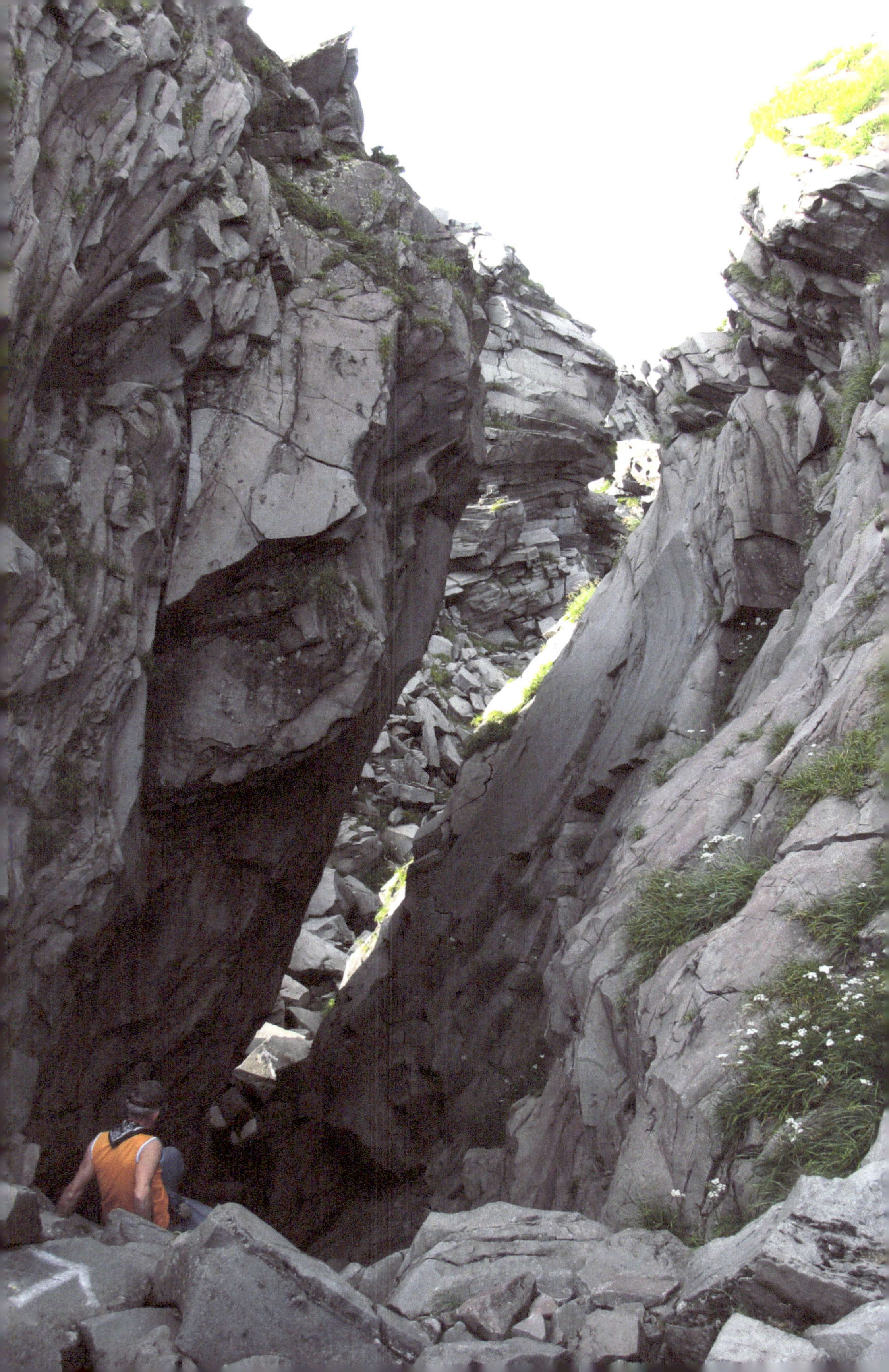

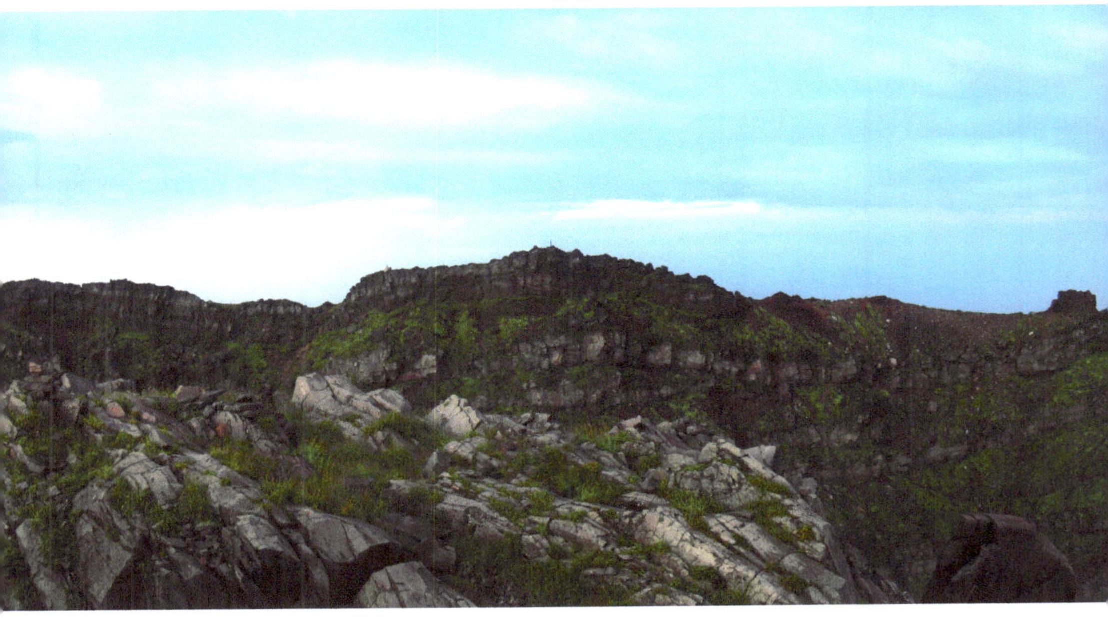

The image above is a two photo panorama taken in 2005, which shows the ridgeline to the east of the Mt. Chokai summit. If you go back to the map on page 11, directly to the east of the summit you will see a peak which has an elevation of 2229.2 meters. The area you see in this panorama is that ridgeline, and if you study the above image very carefully you can even see a wooden post at just about the exact center of the image, which marks its 2229.2 meter summit. We have never hiked over to there. We don't know what the view from that ridge is. We have seen people over there and waved our hands at them, and they have waved back to us, but that's all. Maybe someday we'll go over there.

Now it's time to show you some photos of the summit of Mt. Chokai which we took in 2005 — you may recall that on our first attempt to get to the summit we did not make it — we ended up on one of the many false summits. Therefore, the 2-page spread panoramic image shown on pages 40 and 41 is of the summit of Mt. Chokai (2,236 m = 7,336 ft) which we were able to take from the false summit which we ended up on. The black arrow shows the actual summit. If you study that area closely you can see that there is actually some white writing on that one rock which the arrow points to — that writing identifies it as the summit.

We were disappointed that we did not get to the true summit, but we were able to get to the true summit on the following morning, and we'll show you some morning shots soon.

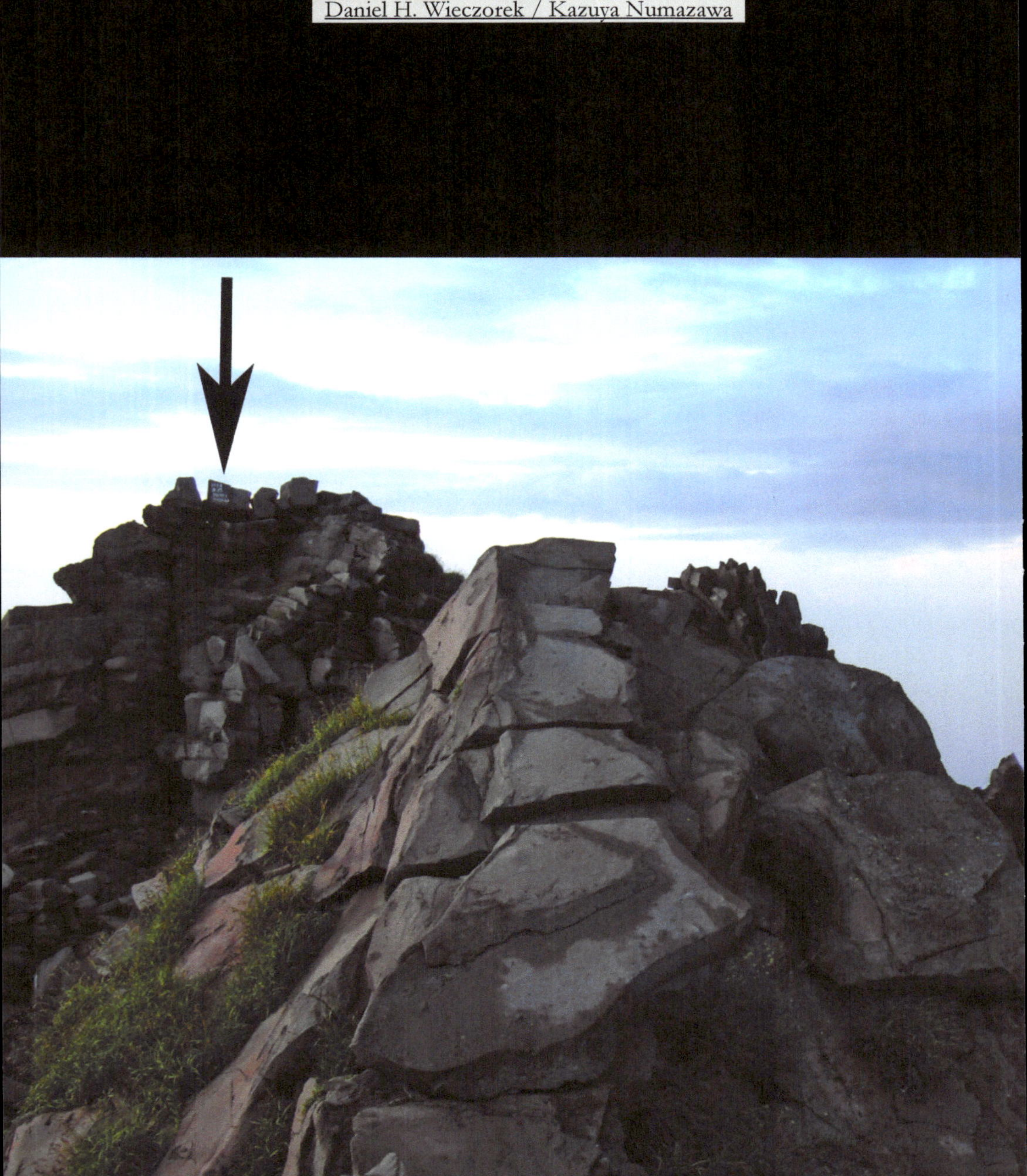

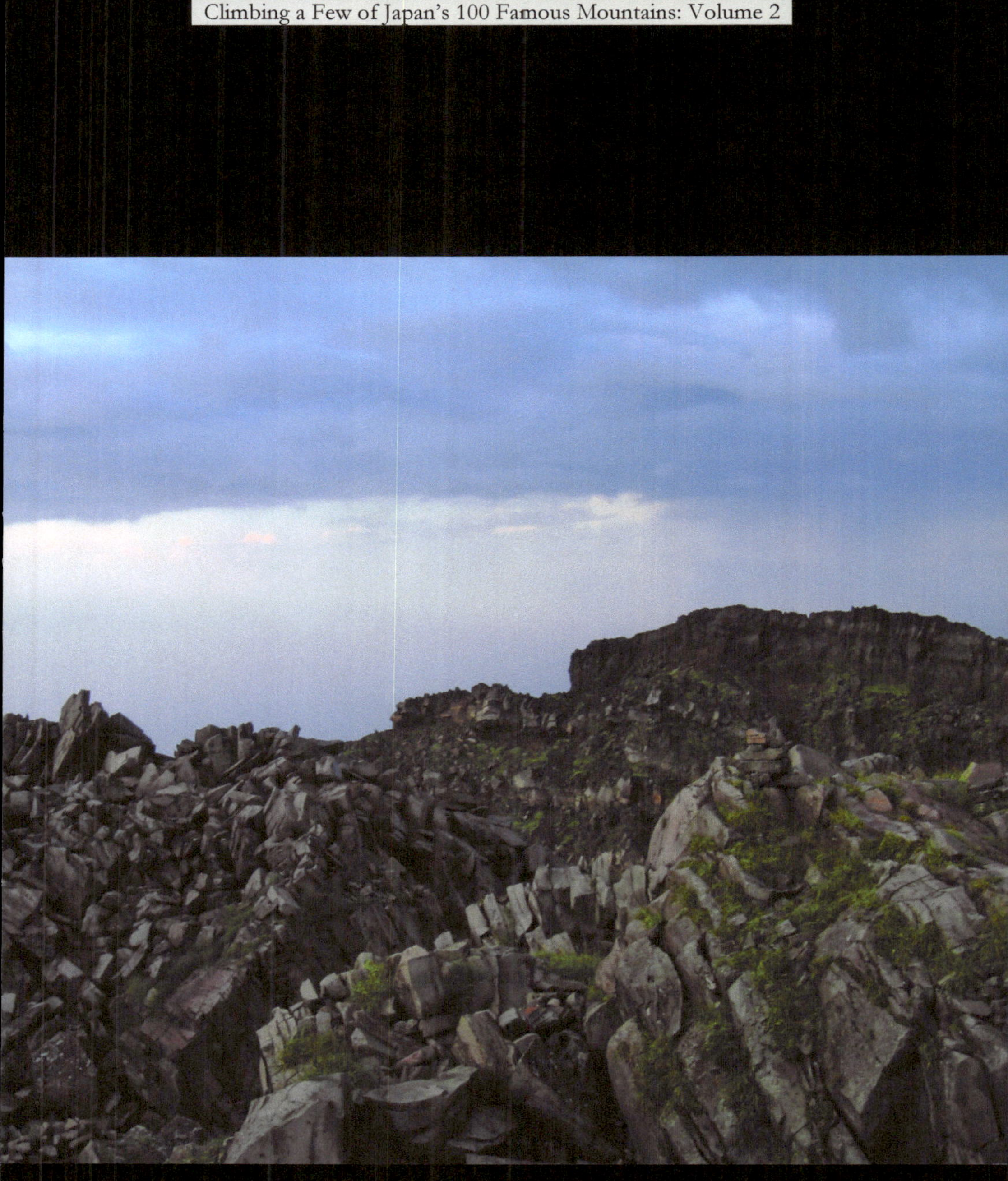

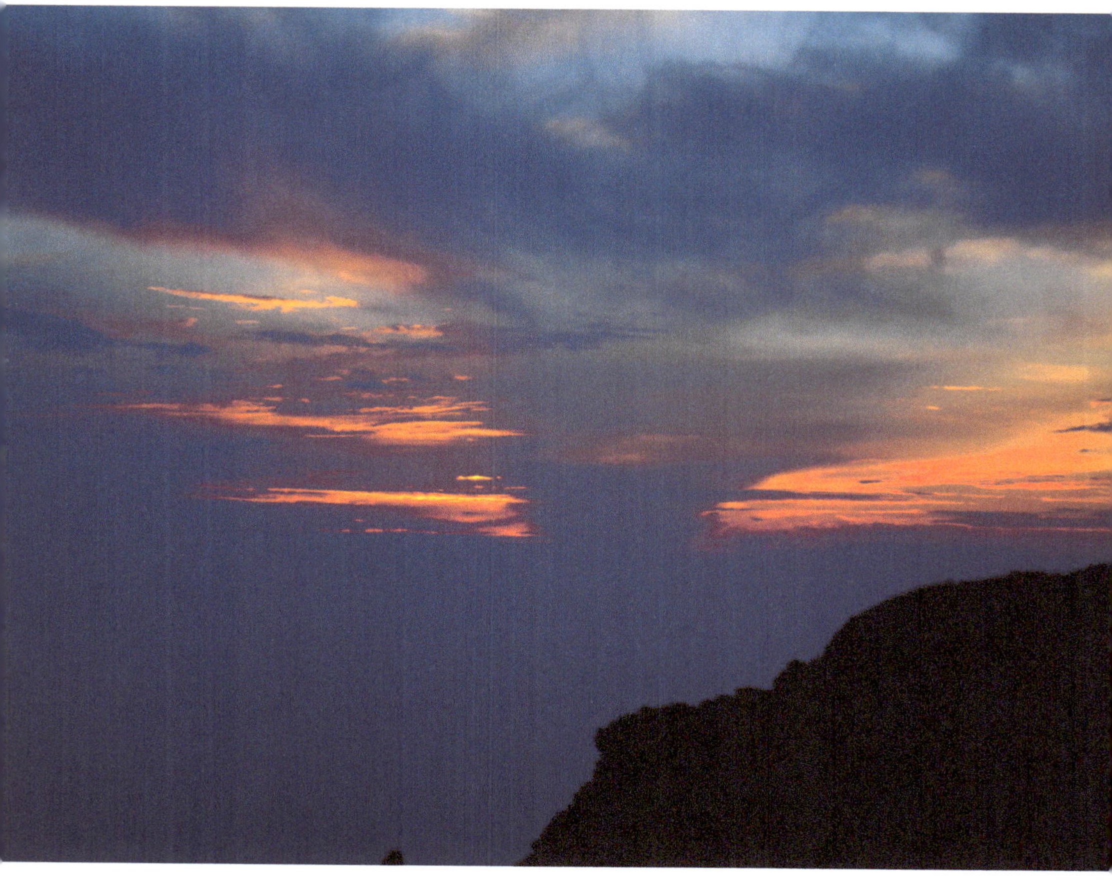

Immediately above is the most interesting sunset photo we captured during our 2005 climb. That's a very interesting cloud which is blocking the sun.

When we climbed this mountain in 2008 we had a better sunset and on the facing page we'll show you two photos of that 2008 sunset hour.

The first photo shows some nice colors and also shows the island of Tobishima, in the sea of Japan. This island is a mere 2.75 square kilometers in area. And, according to sources, it had 275 inhabitants in 2005. You can travel there by scheduled ferry from Sakata, Yamagata Prefecture. Kazuya and I have discussed making a trip out to there several times, but we have never done it. It is located 39 kilometers off the Honshu coast of Japan.

The second photo also shows Tobishima, but that photo is extremely zoomed in and the setting sun offers some nice colors on the surrounding water of the Sea of Japan. Note the small boat.

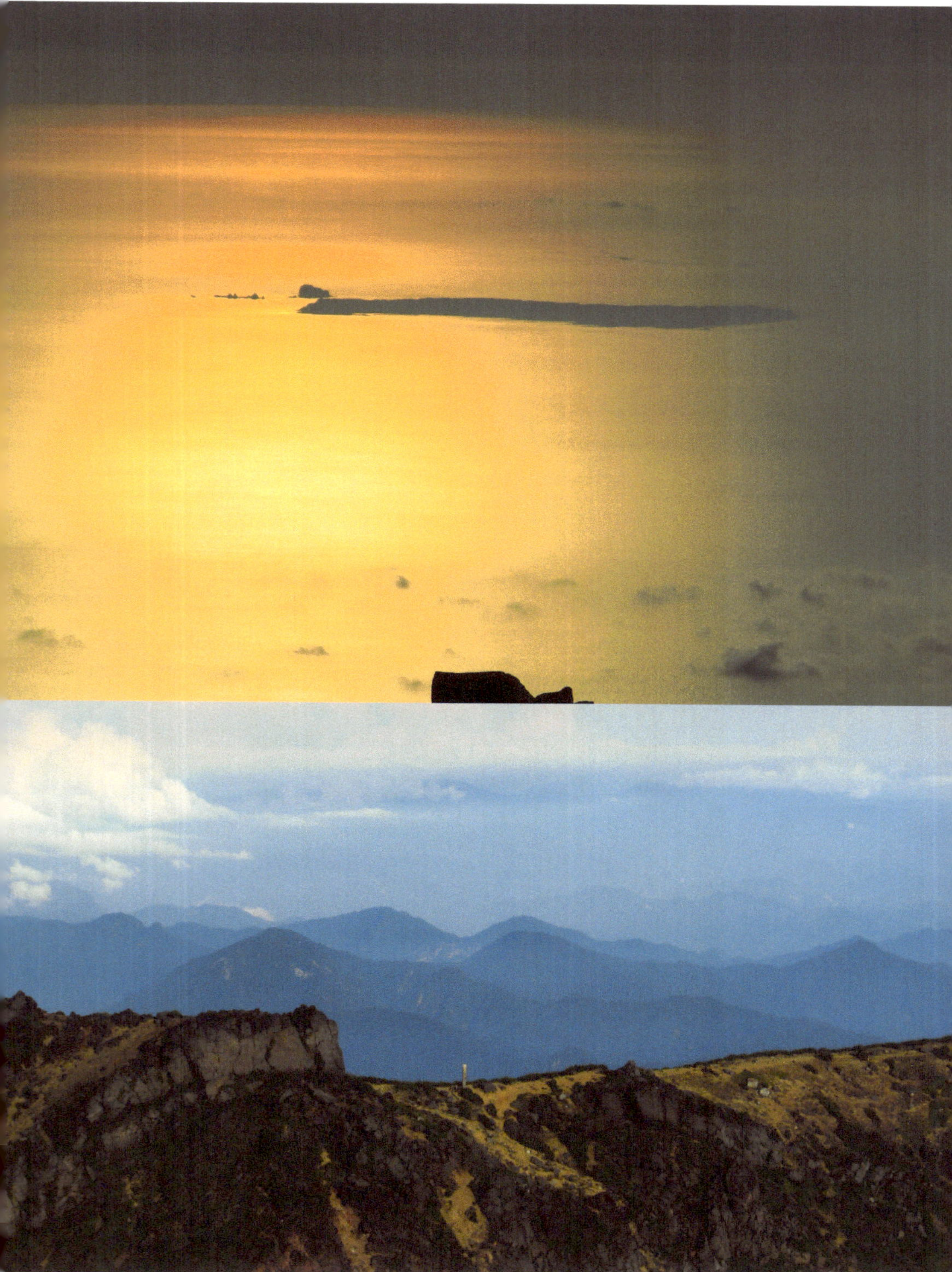

When we climbed in 2011 we were able to witness the most amazing sunset we had yet seen from here and we spent more than an hour on the summit watching the different phases that the setting sun went through. The upper photo on the facing page shows the island of Tobishima with some detail which we were certainly not able to see in 2008.

The lower photo on the facing page shows the same ridgeline as shown on page 39. You will note that when we are on the true summit of Mt. Chokai, and not a false summit, it's possible to see over the top of this ridge.

The two full page spread photos on the following two pages show some additional amazing sights we witnessed in 2011 as the sun was setting. The next two photos show sun dogs. Although sun dogs are not a rare phenomenon, they are always a welcome one to see, and on this day we were given the opportunity to see double sun dogs, that is, one on each side of the sun and 22° distant from it. They lasted for nearly the entire sunset and we took a multitude of photos of them. These are the best ones.

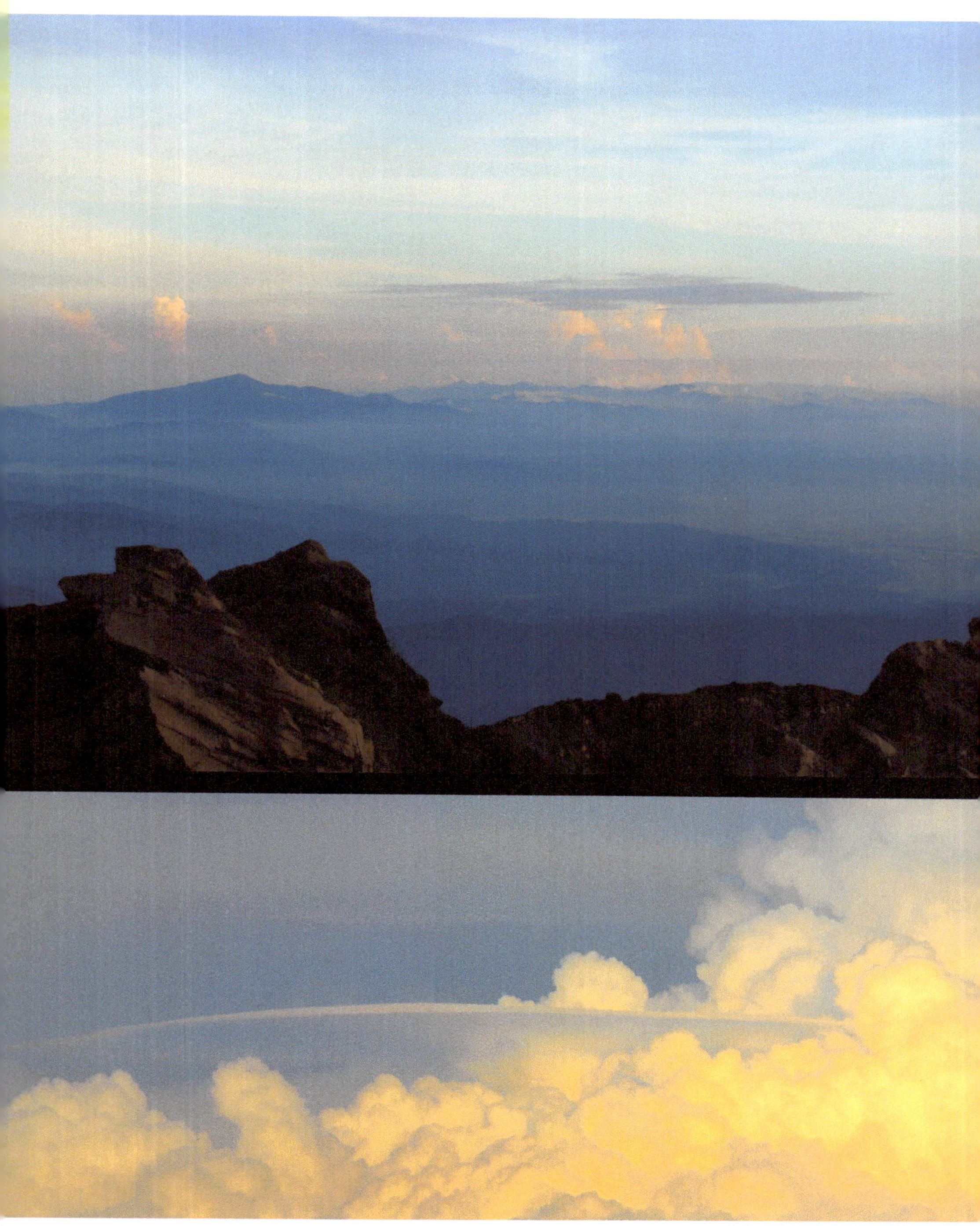

The two photos on the facing page also show sights which we were shown as the sun was setting on August 8, 2011. The upper photo shows the scenery which we were able to see while looking in a generally southerly direction. We had never before been able to see such scenery from here.

The lower photo on the facing page shows another cloud phenomenon which we saw as we spent over an hour at the summit looking around. The thing to ask yourself while looking at this photo is "what is that lenticular cloud doing there mixed in with those cumulus clouds?"

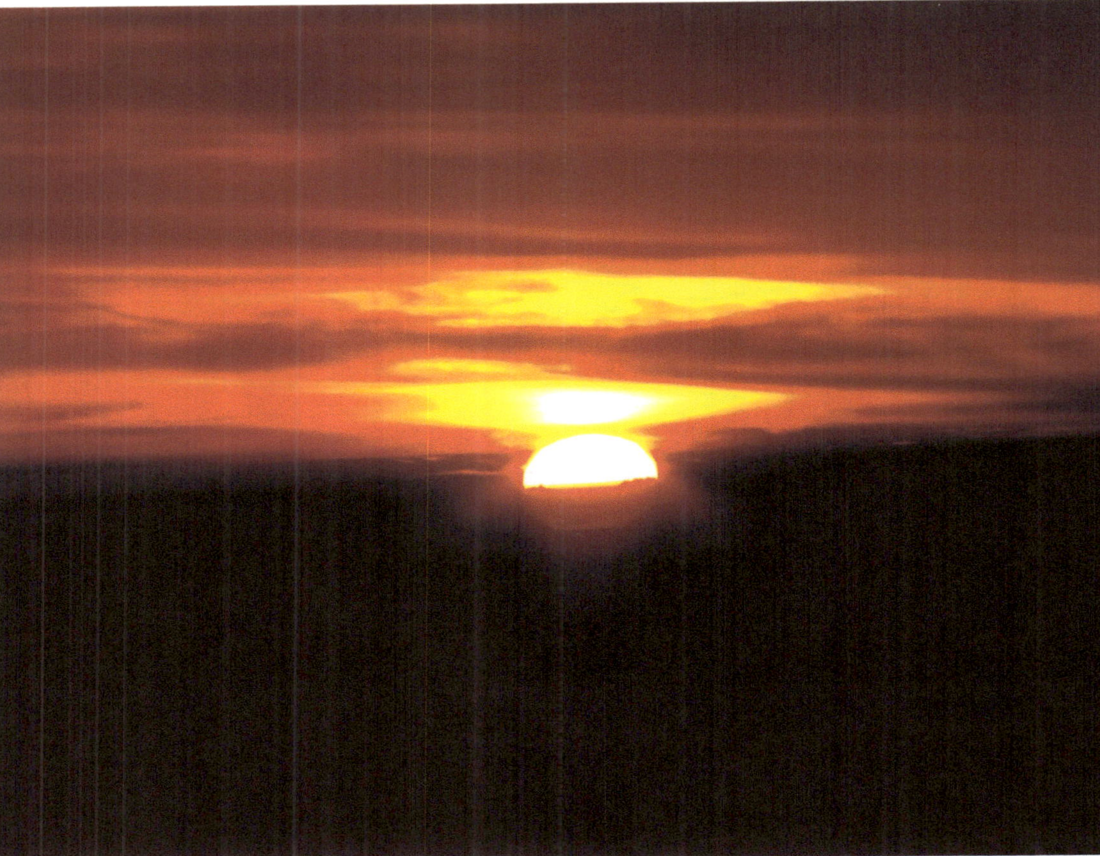

Just above is the final sunset photo from our 2011 climb of Mt. Chokai. This shows the setting sun at 6:51 PM. Could one ask for anything more wonderful?

The photo on the following page shows us at the summit on each of our three climbs of Mt. Chokai with a 2011 sun dog background in the lower portion.

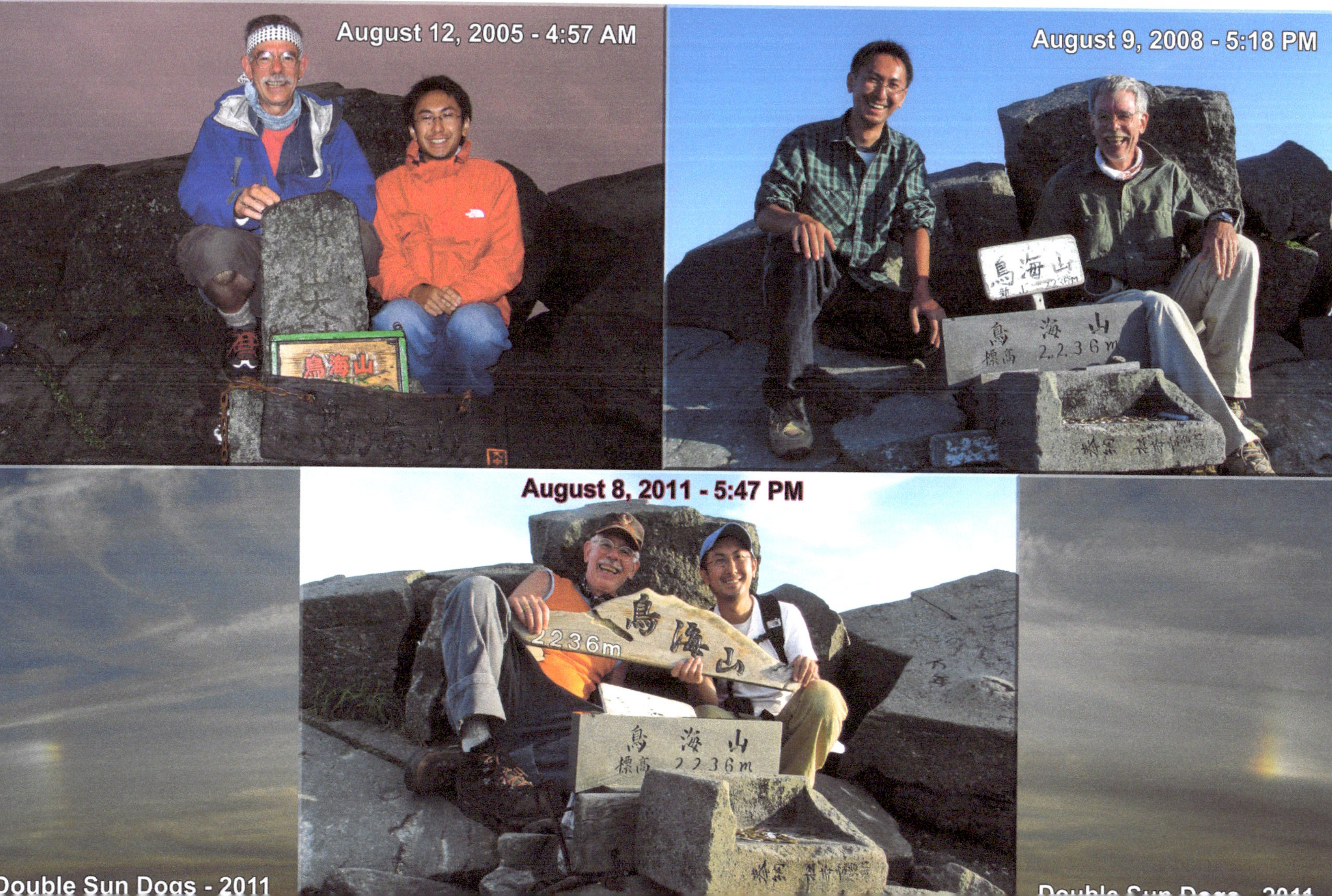

August 12, 2005 - 4:57 AM
August 9, 2008 - 5:18 PM
August 8, 2011 - 5:47 PM
鳥海山
鳥海山
標高 2236m
2236m
鳥海山
鳥海山
標高 2236m
Double Sun Dogs - 2011
Double Sun Dogs - 2011

That ends sunset time in 2011. Now we'll show you some sunrise time photos taken during all three climbs. The photo immediately below was taken at 4:56 AM on August 12, 2005. So, you can deduce that we did not see a great sunrise that year. We had read about the possibility of a beautiful sunrise here and given that, one can see the shadow of this mountain on the Sea of Japan off to the west. Not on this date though.

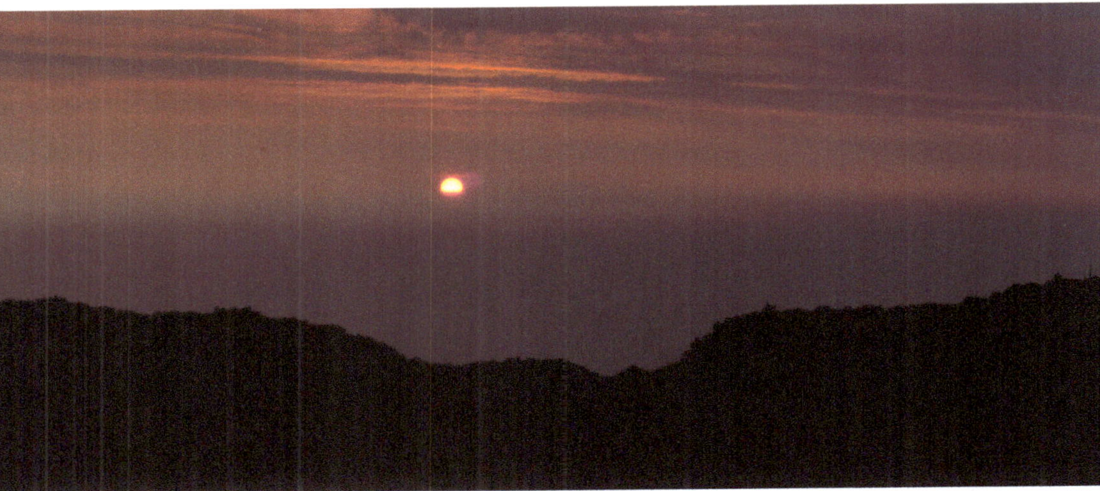

In the photo just below you can see two climbers scrambling for the peak. We took this shot just a very few moments after we had left the peak and were heading back down to the hut.

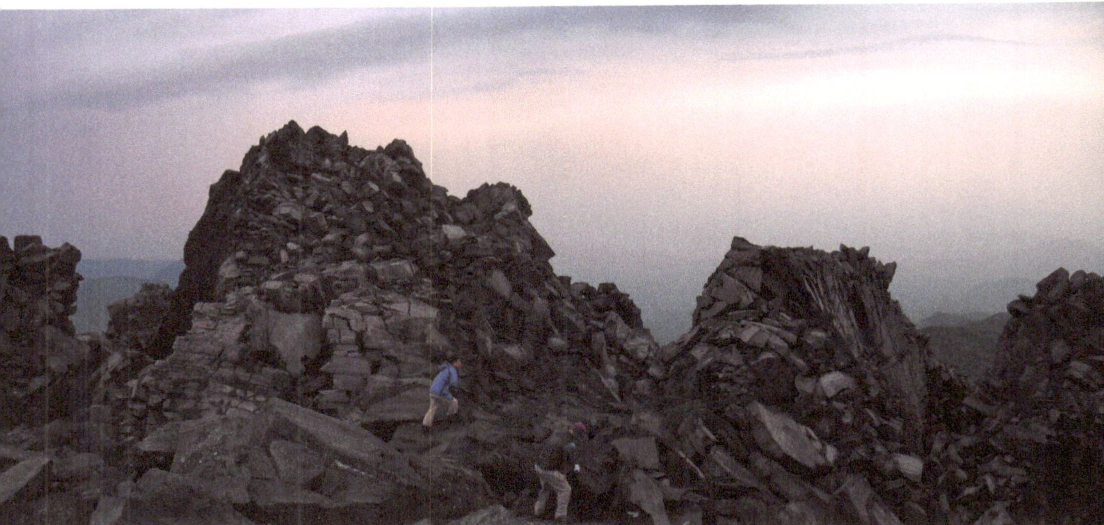

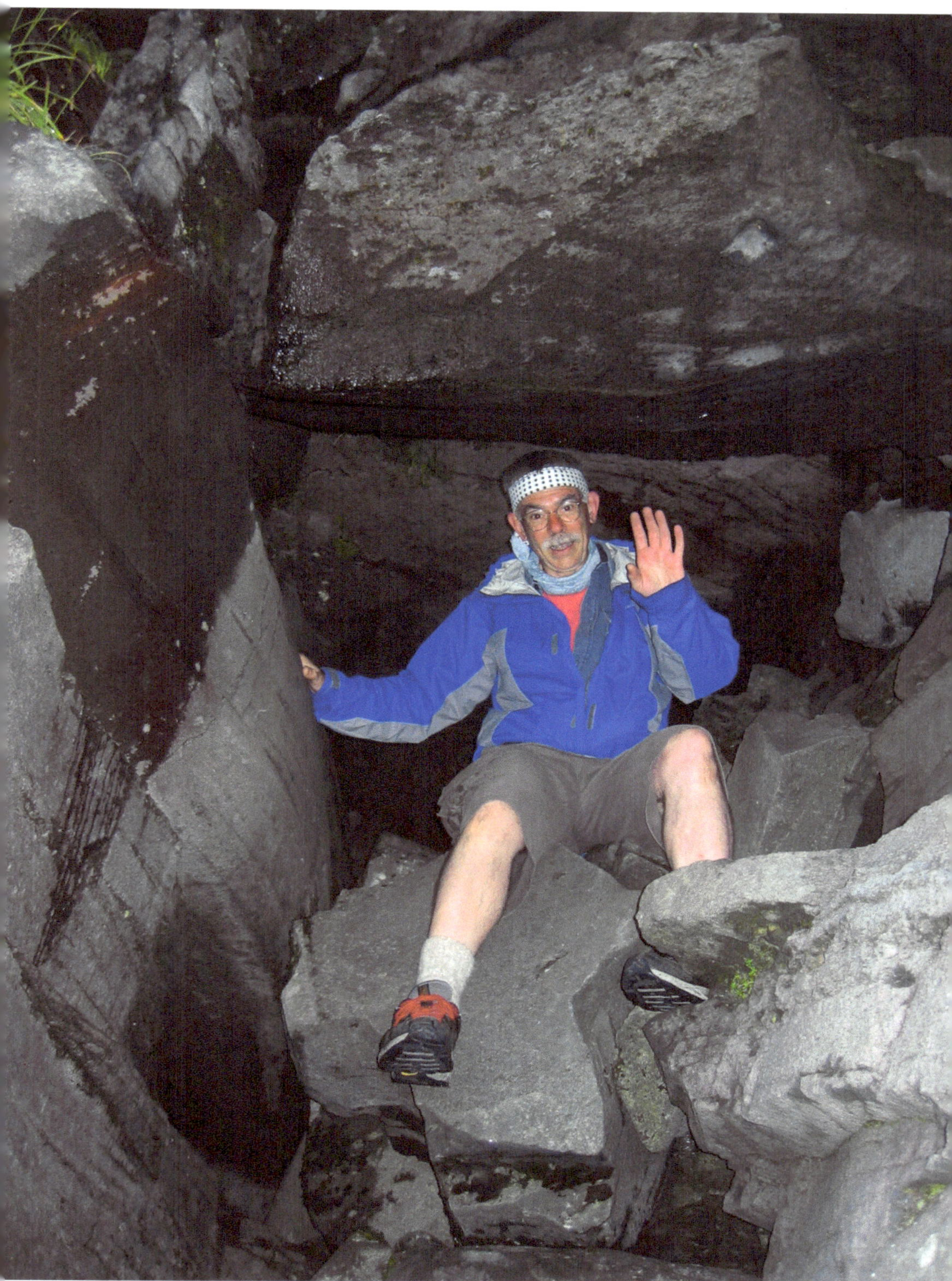

Ha! The photo on the facing page shows me in 2005 as I scramble from the summit back to the hut so that we can eat our breakfast, pack up and leave for the base. If you think my face looks like I am frightened it is only because it is true – this descent is one during which one could be very badly injured if one slipped. You have already seen photos in which you can gauge the size of these boulders, so you know that it certainly could be an easier place to get around. Despite the difficulty of this ascent/descent from the hut to the summit and back, it seems that nearly every person who comes here undertakes it, and most are not at all interested in the sunset, they only want to see the sunrise and, if they are fortunate, the shadow of Mt. Chokai on the Sea of Japan. During that amazing sunset in 2011 when we saw the sun dogs and all of the other beauty, we were the only two people at the summit for the entire time of the setting sun!

When we visited here in 2008 it was raining in the morning and we did not even climb to the summit in the morning.

In 2011 it was beautifully clear and everybody in the hut was up very early and headed for the summit. The summit is not a very large area and we knew that it would be terribly overcrowded, so we did not go to the summit in 2011 either, however, from the area near the hut we had an amazing sunrise time – and at that place we were virtually alone to enjoy it. We dislike crowds very much.

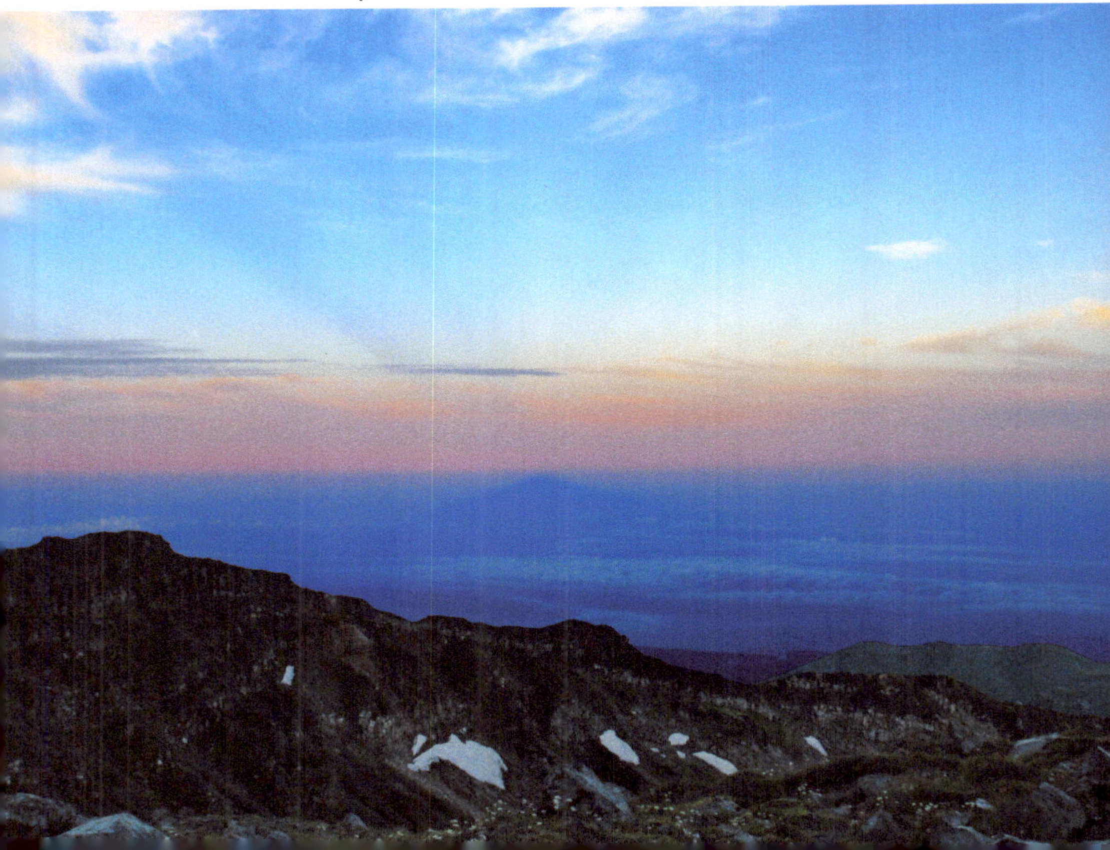

The photo of the shadow of Mt. Chokai on the Sea of Japan on the previous page, taken at 4:50 AM on August 9, 2011, has been lovingly processed with Photoshop® in an attempt to bring out the anti-crepuscular rays which appear to be emanating from the summit of the mountain. In actuality they showed up quite well, but they were not recorded well by either of our digital cameras. This photo shows them fairly well and the manipulation with Photoshop makes them stand out enough to be seen.

This shadow of Mt. Chokai on the sea of Japan is what we had been hoping to be able to witness every time we came here. Apparently the third time was the charm.

The photo below was taken at 5:02 AM on the same day and it shows the shadow increasing in size as the sun gets up a little higher in the sky. We were able to watch this all happen, from the very first hint of a shadow until the sun was high enough in the sky so that the shadow disappeared. All in all it happened over about a twenty minute period. It was such an amazing phenomenon to witness!

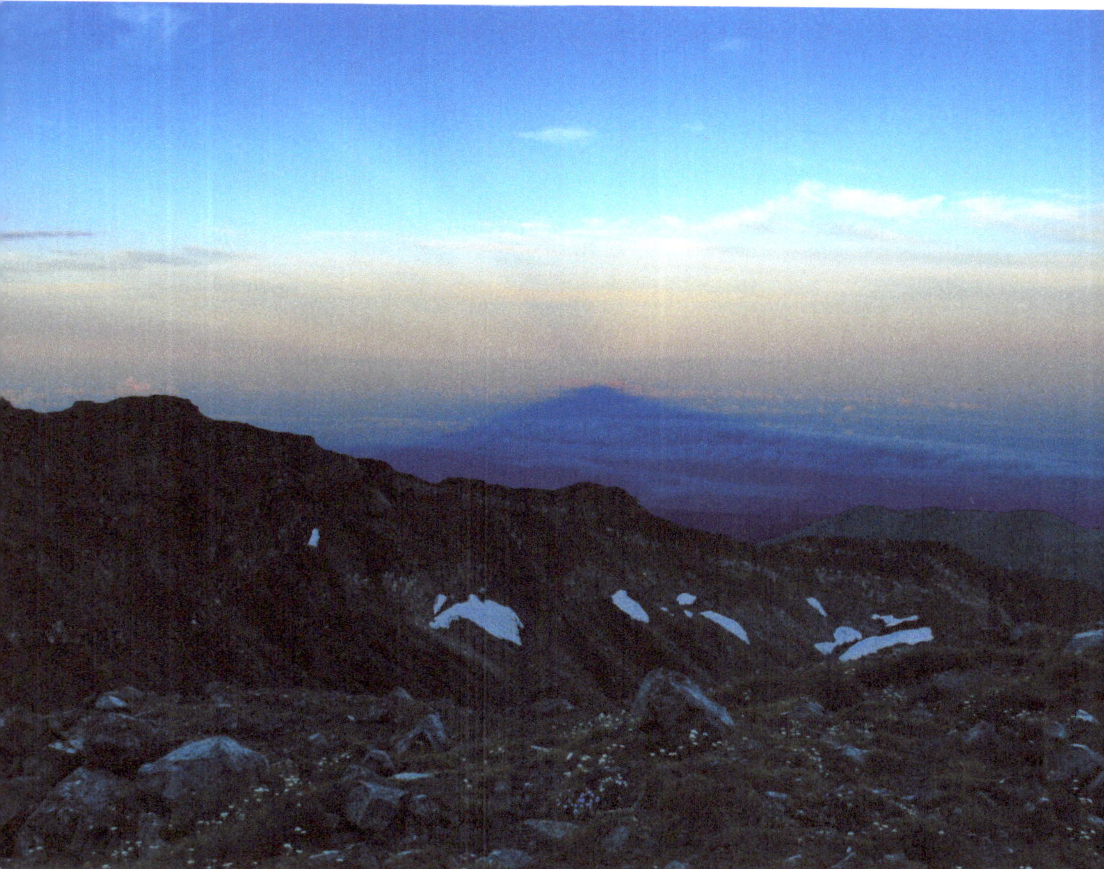

All that remains now are a few photos of descending this amazing mountain. If you take another look at the map back on page 11, we have always descended Mt. Chokai, from the summit hut back to the 2. annotation point via the trail marked with the 4. annotation. That means that the next several photos were taken from along that trail.

The image immediately below is an HDR photo. What does that mean? It means that I took three exposure-bracketed shots – one under-exposed, a correctly exposed one and one overexposed, and then combined them together into a single image using special software. By following this procedure one is able to generally reduce the blackness of deep shadows and the burned out problem of bright sunlight areas. This photo was taken at 6:09 AM, so the shadows in the foreground were still very dark. The problem, however, with HDR images is that it is very difficult to make them appear "photorealistic". I have attempted to do so here by reducing the saturation. The little white dot on the ridge near the center is the hut which is north of the lake (see map).

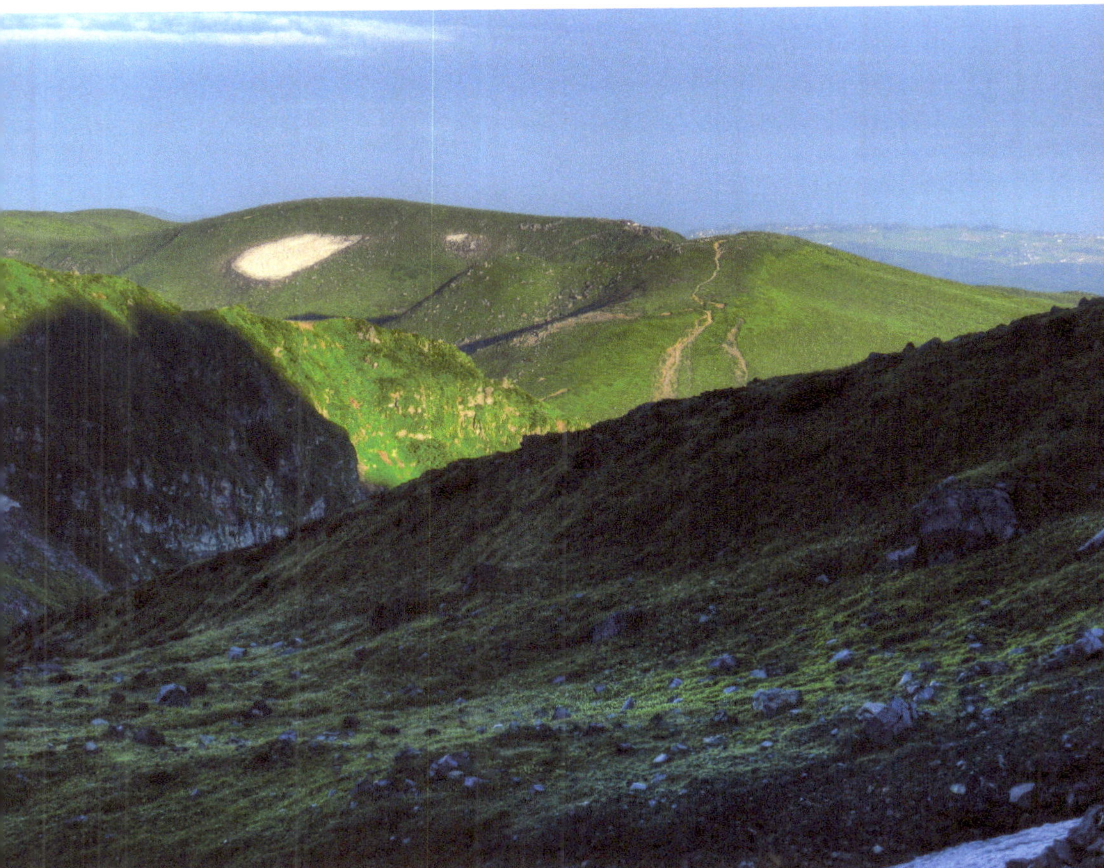

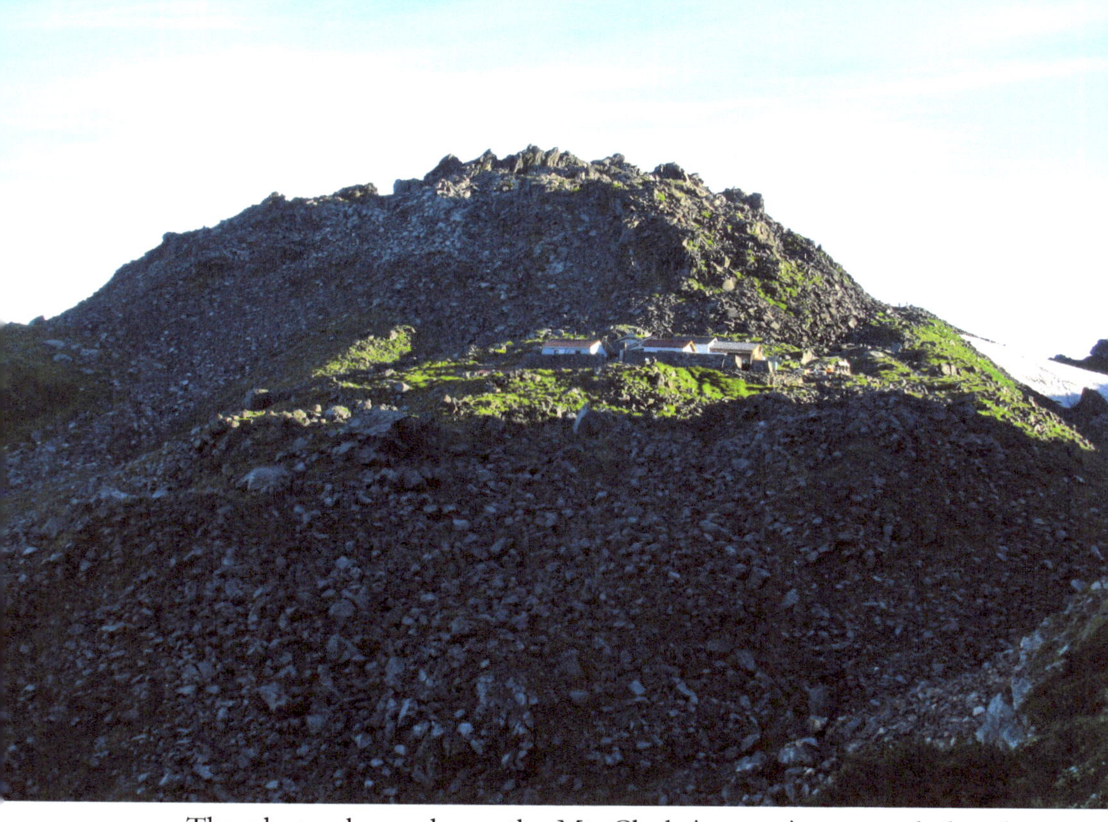

The photo above shows the Mt. Chokai summit area and also the hut and associated buildings. It was taken from the ridge line of the trail marked with the 4. on the map. The time was 6:14 AM (August 9, 2011).

Now, on the facing page we would like to show you some amazingly green slopes. These two photos were taken from the point marked 2005 (meters in elevation) on the ridge-top trail which we are descending the mountain on. They were taken looking to the southwest and absolutely nothing has been done to either one of them to enhance any color shades or the saturation.

The embossed and outlined area in the upper photo marks the approximate area of the lower photo. These photos were taken during our 2008 descent at about 8:15 AM.

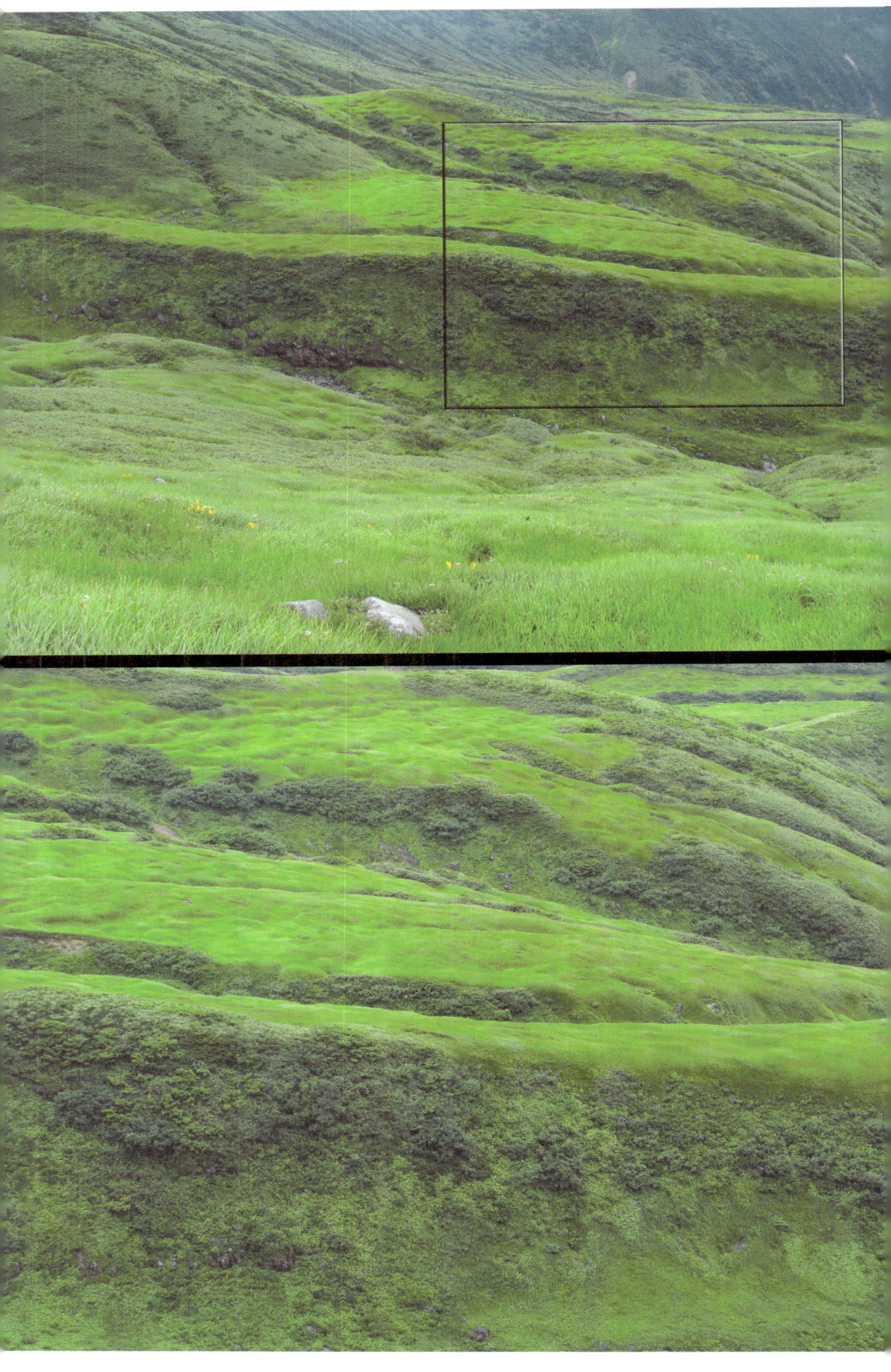

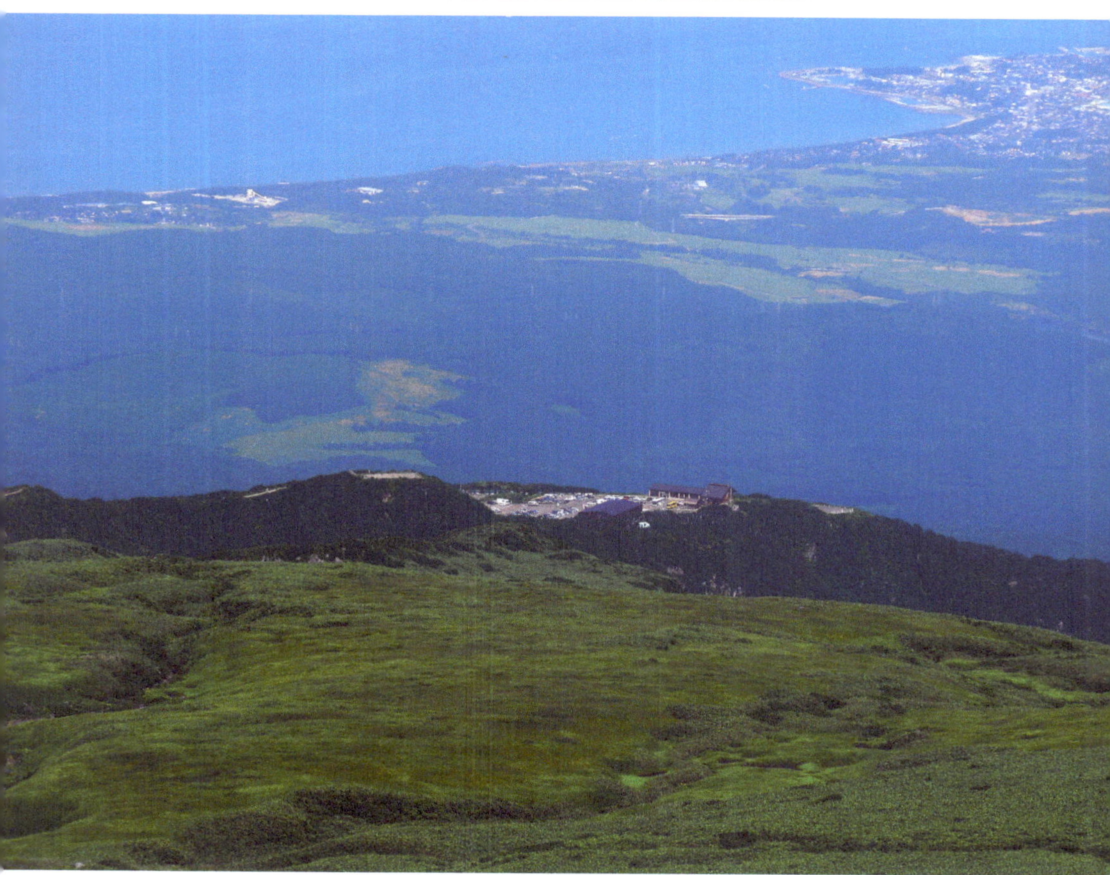

The photo just above was taken during our 2008 descent and in it you can see all the way to the Sea of Japan. You can also see the parking lot down at the starting point (Hokodate). We can't remember precisely where this photo was taken from, but most likely it was also taken very close to the spot on the trail with the 4. annotation (see map, page 11), which says 2005 (which is the elevation in meters of the peak called Mon-judake (文珠岳). What a great view!

The upper photo on the facing page was taken on August 9, 2011 at 6:24 AM; it shows the beautiful scenery we were able to see when looking more or less south from near that same point at Monjudake (文珠岳).

The lower photo on the facing page shows more mountain scenery and it's very likely that the mountain which you see to the right of center is Mt. Gassan (1,984 m = 6,509 ft), which will be the mountain we take you to in Volume 3 of this series of books.

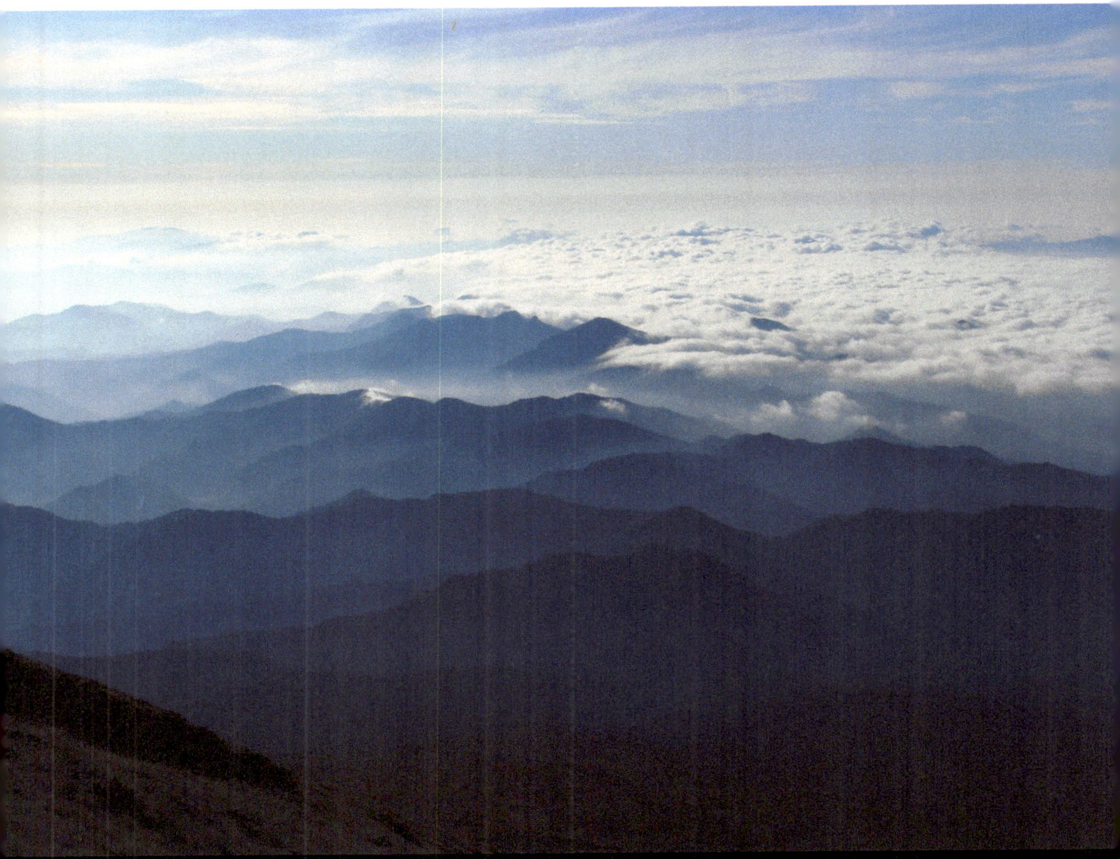

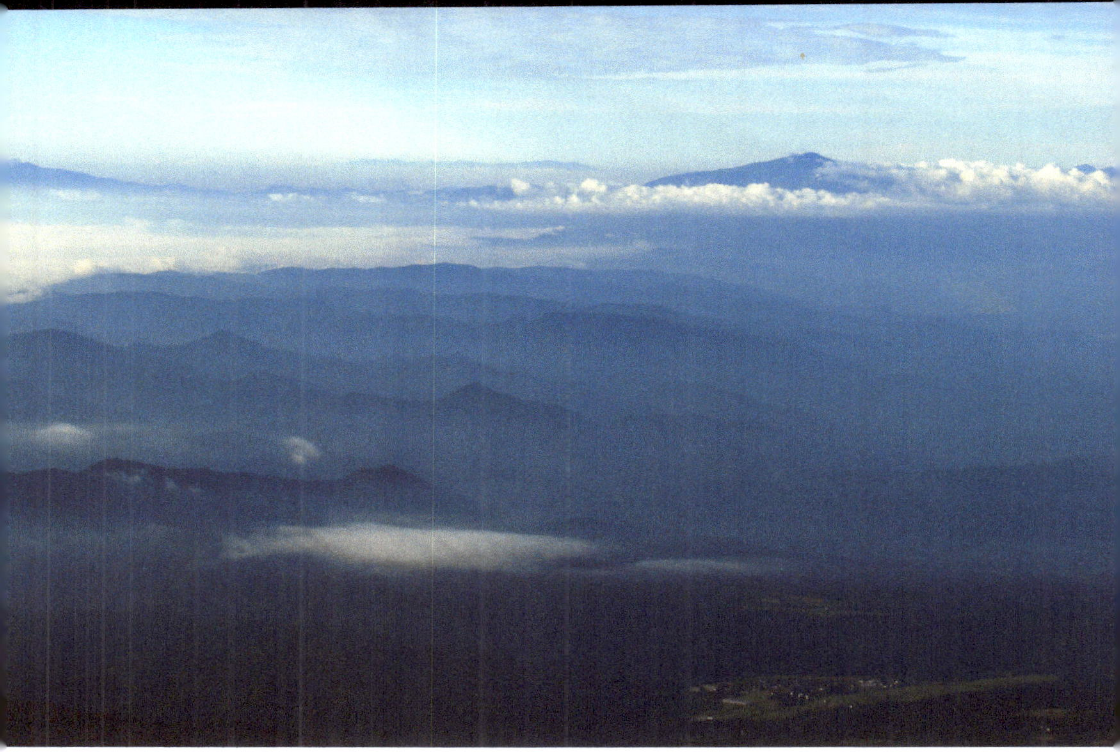

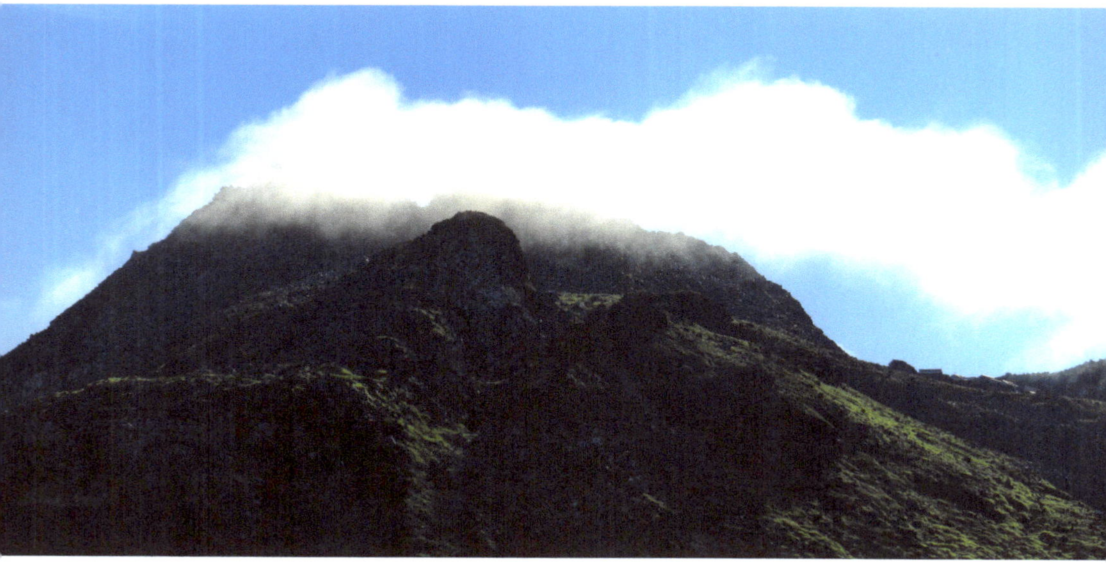

The photo immediately above shows the peak of Mt. Chokai at 7:30 AM on August 9, 2011. Strange how this cloud happened to form right at the peak. It was not there five minutes before this, and it was gone five minutes later.

The next, and final photo for this, Volume 2, shows Mt. Chokai as we rode on the train to the east from Sakata, Yamagata Prefecture. This photo was taken at 3:35 PM, also on August 9, 2011.

We hope you enjoyed your armchair adventure nearly as much as we enjoyed our three climbs of this mountain. Volume 3 will take us, as stated above, to Mt. Gassan (1,984 m = 6,509 ft) (月山), also in Yamagata Prefecture.

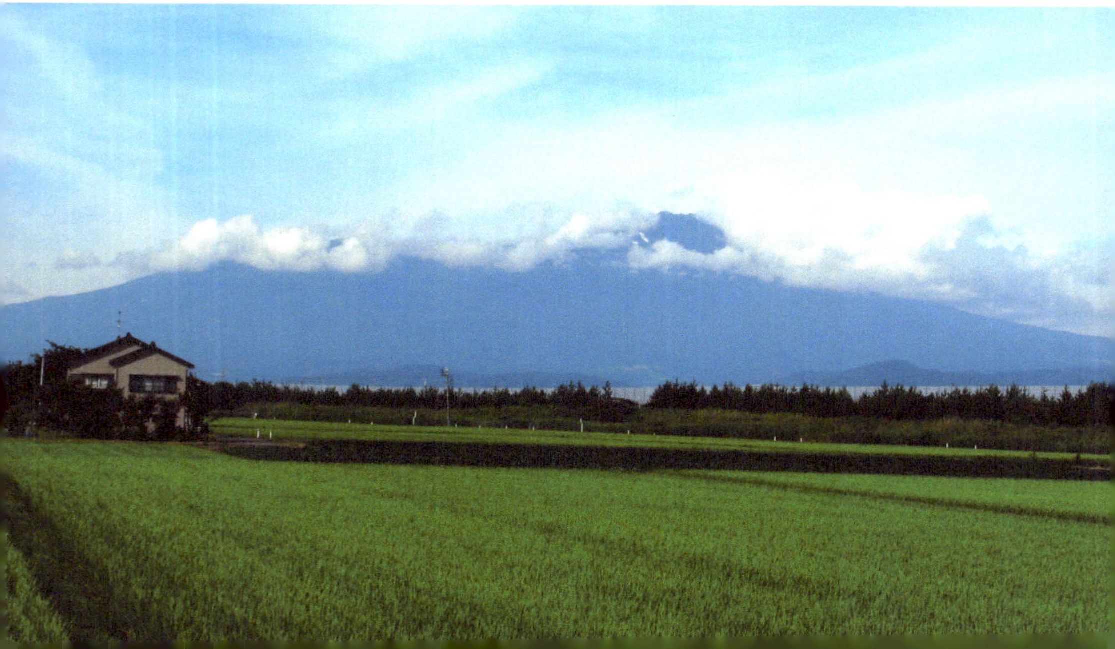

We sincerely hope that you are enjoying this series of books. If you would like any further information about any of these mountains there is a great abundance of it available on the internet.

If you want to e-mail me with specific questions you may do so through the link on my website, which is http://danwiz.com. I hope to maintain this site as long as I am alive.

THE END

ABOUT THE AUTHORS

Daniel Wieczorek was born in 1947 in Ionia, Michigan. He graduated from the University of Michigan with a B.S. in Forestry in 1969. He moved to Oregon to work in the field of forestry in 1971. That was followed by a move to Alaska in 1975, where he continued his career in forestry. After about a 14 year career in forestry, Daniel decided to do something different and he served as a Peace Corps Volunteer in The Philippines from 1985 – 1987. Upon completion of his Peace Corps service he returned to Alaska, where he attended the University of Alaska – Fairbanks and received an M.B.A. in 1991. This was followed by a move to South Korea in 1992, where Daniel taught English to Korean people wishing to improve their English Language skills. Daniel's next stop was in New York City, where he worked as temporary staff at Deutsche Bank from 1998 – 2001. He left NYC in March 2001 and moved on to his present home in Mitaka City, Tokyo, Japan. He is teaching English in Japan and at this time he's been teaching as a career for about 17 years. He has been hiking, climbing and doing photography since he was about 12 years old.

Kazuya Numazawa was born in 1979 in Shinjo in Yamagata Prefecture, Japan. He was raised in Funagata Town in Yamagata Prefecture. He graduated from Tokyo University in 2005. Since that time he has worked in several fields, but primarily in Cram Schools around the Mitaka Area.

Daniel and Kazuya met in 2001 and they have been hiking, mountain climbing and doing photography together since that time and generally enjoying life together.

NOTES

PHOTO CREDITS

Daniel's Photos:

Pages 10 bottom, 11, 13 all, 14 all, 15 all, 16, 18 all, 19, 21, 22 all, 23, 24, 25 all, 26, 27, 28, 30-31, 32 top, 33 top, 35, 36, 39, 40-41, 42, 43 all, 44 all, 46-47, 48 all, 49, 50, 51 all, 53, 54, 55, 56, 57 all, 58, 59 all, 60 all.

Kazuya's Photos:

Pages 9, 10 top, 12, 17, 20 all, 29, 32 bottom, 33 bottom, 34, 35 top, 37, 38, 52.